Every young lady desiring to be married one day must read this book! It will challenge you; it will stir you; it will delight you! Most importantly, it will help you practically prepare for one of the most important decisions of your life. In *Before You Meet Prince Charming*, Sarah Mally tackles the most critical subject for single women and offers insightful counsel with a wonderful sense of humor. I believe this will be a great encouragement to princesses everywhere!

—Beall Phillips
WIFE OF DOUG PHILLIPS, PRESIDENT OF VISION FORUM

Sarah Mally is a "bright light" in our day—a winsome, counter-cultural young woman with a passion for Christ and for truth. I am thankful for the way God is using her, and for her vision to reflect and point others to the beauty of Christ and His ways.

—Nancy Leigh DeMoss
AUTHOR, HOST OF REVIVE OUR HEARTS RADIO

Christians are called to be the light of the world. In an age of increasing moral pollution and defilement, the world desperately needs the enlightenment, exposure and radiant joy of Christian purity. And nowhere should this light shine more brightly than in the radiant purity of Christian young ladies. Sarah Mally has a special ministry that has blessed thousands of girls throughout the United States and a special God-given gift of inspiring them to a closer walk with their Lord. I wholeheartedly endorse her call to radiant purity.

—Roger Magnuson, Esq.
DEAN OF OAKBROOK COLLEGE OF LAW,
FOUNDER AND PREACHING ELDER OF STRAITGATE CHURCH

As soon as I started reading Sarah's book I knew it was a message that girls today desperately need to understand. Through an enchanting fairytale it encourages them to take a courageous stand for purity, to guard their hearts and minds, and to shine brightly in their generation.

—Sheri Prescott
AUTHOR AND SPEAKER, *Iowa* (1997)

In *Before You Meet Prince Charming*, Miss Sarah Mally tells a sweet and delightfully humorous story of a young princess and her longing to meet and marry her own true prince. Woven throughout are godly principles to help guide and protect any woman in her quest to know, wait for, and follow God's plan for a modern courtship and marriage. Creatively accomplished and very helpful.

—Gregg Harris

AUTHOR OF *THE CHRISTIAN HOME SCHOOL*
FATHER BEHIND WWW.THEREBELUTION.COM

Sarah Mally is like a loving "big sis" to a generation of girls whose perceptions of love and romance have been seriously distorted by a culture intent on breaking their hearts. *Before You Meet Prince Charming* answers the big questions in a friendly, honest, and light-hearted fashion. We are adding it to our "courtship" reading list with pleasure.

—Dr. Jeff and Danielle Myers

AUTHOR AND SPEAKER, FOUNDER OF MYERS INSTITUTE

Before You Meet Prince Charming fills a niche in contemporary Christian literature that is much needed today. From her own heart and experience, Sarah Mally encourages and exhorts young Christian girls who are morally pure and protected to wait on the Lord for His choices in marriage and ministry. Many of the emotional pitfalls that these godly girls will face as they mature into womanhood are exposed and discussed in this well written and easy to read book. Using a literary style that combines an allegory set in medieval times with straight to the point commentary, the author challenges young Christian girls to remain pure and faithful. Humorous illustrations, memory verses and practical assignments make *Before You Meet Prince Charming* a good choice for use in small groups.

—Dr. David R. Reid

AUTHOR, FOUNDER AND DIRECTOR OF GROWING CHRISTIANS MINISTRIES,
FORMER FACULTY MEMBER OF EMMAUS BIBLE COLLEGE

BEFORE YOU MEET PRINCE CHARMING

CHARMING

A Guide to Radiant Purity

BEFORE YOU MEET PRINCE CHARMING

CHARMING

A Guide to Radiant Purity

By SARAH MALLY

Story Illustrations by Dan Brandon
Cartoons by Brandon Weaver

Tomorrow's Forefathers

Before You Meet Prince Charming
Copyright © 2006 by Sarah Mally

Published by
    Tomorrow's Forefathers, Inc.
    PO Box 11451
    Cedar Rapids, Iowa 52410-1451

Production arrangements by
    Winters Publishing
    PO Box 501
    Greensburg, Indiana 47240
    800-457-3230

Cover design: Jeremy Fisher
Cover illustration: Dan Brandon
Cover photo: Stephen Mally
Story illustrations: Dan Brandon
Cartoons: Brandon Weaver

First printing 2006, Second printing 2006, Third Printing 2007
Printed in the United States of America

Unless otherwise noted, Scripture references are from the King James Version.

Scripture marked NASB is taken from the New American Standard Bible®, Copyright © 1960, 1962, 1963, 1968, 1971, 1972, 1973, 1975, 1977, 1995 by The Lockman Foundation. Used by permission.

Library of Congress Control Number: 2006901586
ISBN-10: 0-9719405-4-1
ISBN-13: 978-0-9719405-4-3

Dedicated to all the young ladies in Bright Lights. May you shine with radiant purity as you remember that you are true princesses of the heavenly King.

Table of Contents

With Gratefulness:

Dad, you are my knight in shining armor! This book would never have been possible without you. Your wisdom, protection, vision for ministry, and unwavering commitment to the Lord have provided the best example and Biblical foundation for my life that I could have ever asked for. Thank you for the many, many hours you spent helping with graphics and editing. I love working with you!

Mom, you are the most encouraging person I know! Thank you for taking care of so many details so that I could concentrate on this book. Since the day I was born, you have been an example to me of a godly wife and taught me what it means to live for Christ. Your help, encouragement, and advice made a huge difference to me as I was working on this project!

Stephen, thank you for making my life so much fun, and for your loyalty, great advice, and commitment to seeking first the kingdom of God. Thank you for being my personal computer technician and for all the time you have put into the layout and many other details of this book! I appreciate your commitment to quality and your great sense of humor!

Grace, thank you for being the sweetest sister in the world. All the special extra things you do add lots of happiness and many special memories to each day. Thank you for all your help with editing, and for your radiant example of seeking Jesus with all of your heart.

A Special Thanks to:

Dan Brandon for your fantastic artwork. I know that many hours of thought and work went into each picture. Our family is so thankful to see how God brought our paths together so that we could share with you and you could share with us. Many others will be impacted and blessed because of your work and the sacrifices you have made for Christ's kingdom.

Brandon Weaver for working extra hard at the last minute to get the cartoons finished on time. Grace and I laugh every time we look through your drawings. We enjoy your creativity and humor, and appreciate the way you go the extra mile by thinking about little details.

Jeremy Fisher for your great job on the cover design. You have been super to work with! We appreciate your expertise, flexibility, gracious encouragement, and sensitivity to our goals.

Winters Publishing for your friendship, advice, proofreading, and for being available to assist whenever we need help. We continue to be thankful to the Lord for the way He arranged for us to get acquainted and for how you have met so many of our printing needs!

Grandpa and Grandma Rodgers for laying a godly foundation for our family, and for sacrificing in so many ways to help and support us in our family ministry. Your proofreading, love, encouragement, and prayers mean a lot to me!

All my friends who helped with proofreading: Chrissy Baskerville, Nickie Biegler, Laura Chandler, Amy Cook, Elizabeth Cook, Faith Coventon, Catherine Goodman, Dr. Larry Guthrie, Katy Harris, Claudia Juhl, Steve Knapp, Rebekah May, Lena Mays, Acacia Philipps, Beall Phillips, Donna Rees, Evelyn Talmage, Sandy Wickert, and Phyllis Winters.

Note from the Author:

Over the past eight or nine years, my dad and I have been speaking together on the topic of purity. I often receive questions from mothers about what books I would suggest for their daughters on this subject. Even though there are many good books on romance and purity, I have had difficulty finding one to recommend to younger girls who are pure and protected. Many of the books I have read seem to be written specifically to reach young people who have already made mistakes. Since they are written for this audience, they include some details that I don't think are necessary for younger girls to be thinking about. Even though my desire is that this book would minister to girls of all ages and backgrounds, I have endeavored to keep it discreet and appropriate for younger girls as well.

Note to the lover of Old English: it is not my intent to duplicate proper Old English. Please bear with my inconsistency and incomplete usage, as it is my desire to give only an Old English flavor.

Names and minor details have been altered in some stories for the sake of privacy.

I suggest that parents may want to read this book together with their daughter and discuss each chapter with her. *Before You Meet Prince Charming* is also recommended for small group Bible studies, Sunday school classes, and Bright Lights groups.

May the Lord bless you richly as you seek God's very best and as you purpose to shine with radiant purity.

CHAPTER ONE

Desire the Very Best Marriage

*"Let us be glad and rejoice, and give honor to Him:
for the marriage of the Lamb is come,
and His wife hath made herself ready."*
Revelation 19:7

"Come on, Victory," *the sixteen-year-old girl said softly as she mounted her faithful horse and began the journey to the castle. Her blonde hair, highlighted by the sun, flowed behind her, and the crystals on her thin golden headband sparkled brightly. Cantering gracefully with his dark mane waving in the wind, the chestnut horse was nearly as beautiful as the girl. As they raced across green meadows colored by wildflowers, over small streams, and through the countryside, many people would stop their activities or conversations in order to watch them pass.*

"A lovely girl," one elderly lady commented as she was hanging out linens to dry. "A precious gem, if ever there was one, I say."

A jolly old man sat on a bench in the mountain village with his young grandson by his knee. As the girl rode by, he turned to his grandson and declared, "You do know who she is, do ye not? She is none other but the daughter of the king."

"Then she is a princess, Grandfather?" asked the little boy with wonder and delight, his eyes gazing at her until she had disappeared into the distance.

"Ahh, but she is more than a princess," the wise grandmother who stood nearby interjected. "For not only is she a princess in lineage, but she is also a princess in conduct. We may admire her outward beauty, but I tell you that it is her inner beauty that is worth one hundred times more—and inner beauty is a quality rare even among princesses."

And so you see, this young lady was known and respected throughout the kingdom not only because of her royal birth, but even more importantly for her kindness, gracious words, and evident maturity beyond her years. No one doubted that she was a princess indeed.

Yet, lest you begin to believe that this princess was perfect, it must be noted that even though she was wise, she was not as wise as her father, the king. She was young. She had much insight and discernment, but she was nonetheless still subject to the emotions, fears, and longings that tug and pull at a girl's heart and mind. It was not easy to recall her father's words of wisdom in every situation. And sometimes the wrong advice of others was quite persuasive, sounding so close to the truth that it was easy to accept without due caution.

"I wonder," the princess thought aloud as she reached the top of the small hill from which the castle came into view, "why Father speaks so often of the dangerous ways and opinions of the people in the kingdom. They seem so peaceful and good."

"And I wonder," she continued, "what my future will hold? I suppose Mother is right. It is not for me to know. I must concentrate on the work that God gives me to do each day and trust Him to direct my paths."

"We'd best hurry," she said again to Victory as she gently pressed her legs against his sides. She realized that they had slowed their pace

considerably. Peering into the distant sky, the princess noticed that it seemed strangely dark, and she wondered if it was already past the dinner hour.

Resuming her thoughts, she spoke again. "If the biggest enemies of the kingdom are not the seen but the unseen, and if the villagers are as easily led astray as Father says, I wonder what can be done in order to—"

Suddenly hearing the sound of galloping, she forgot her questions and looked up to see a horseman coming quickly to meet her.

"How does it fare with thee, my lady?" he asked, coming to a halt.

"All is well, sentinel," she replied. "What be thy hurry?"

"Thy father sent me to look for thee. The western sky gives warning of a brewing storm. He was concerned that thou hadst been delayed at Sand Crossing."

"Thou knowest how it is visiting Aunt Prudent and Uncle Justheart, the Duke and Duchess of Wisdomton," she chuckled. "It is always difficult to get away. And yes, the ride home took longer than expected. The rough parts of the mountain trail are somewhat overgrown. Also, I stopped to help an elderly lady who had dropped her basketful of vegetables in the midst of the path."

"I will report to the king and leave thee to enjoy thy quiet ride. Thy father will be glad to know that thou hast very nearly arrived at the castle."

"Thank you, sentinel," she answered. "Please tell the stable hand to have hay ready for Victory."

"As thou sayest," he declared as he turned around and galloped away.

You may be wondering why a princess was riding alone throughout the kingdom with no guards or escort. It was a time of peace, and the land was well protected by the many good knights and warriors scattered throughout. In addition, the king desired that the princess follow not the custom of royalty, who isolate themselves from the common people, but rather that she learn to serve and minister to everyone from the greatest down to the least. He knew that the kingdom was in need of such examples.

Yet, the king was by no means negligent to protect his daughter. On the contrary, because of his great love for the princess, he was committed to doing everything necessary to safeguard her in every way. Indeed, many considered him to be too careful. He often perceived as dangerous those activities that most people believed were quite harmless. And many times he took precautions that others mocked as extreme and unnecessary. For you see, in his wisdom he understood that it was not the outward threats that were most deadly, but the inward pollutants and evil influences that attack the heart and the mind.

The princess, walking by faith, happily accepted this protection and guidance. Even so, it is questionable whether she fully treasured this most valuable gift bestowed upon her. She loved her parents, but it is unlikely that she had a full understanding of what a significant part they played in her life. She appreciated their protection and occasionally thanked them for it, but it is certain that she did not have any idea how much this protection would benefit her life, how vital it was for her future, and how much grief it had already spared her.

Like most princesses, this young lady was full of hopes and dreams for her future. There were places she wished to visit, people she hoped to meet, and great things she wanted to accomplish. Most of all, she desired to use her life to nourish and strengthen others. For you see, she understood (as few princesses do) that a true princess is actually a servant. But amidst her many noble dreams, the one most deeply rooted in her heart and the one she thought of most frequently, was ... (you'll never guess) ... yes, she dreamed of the day when she would fall in love with her Prince Charming and live with him forever. But, of course, she was only sixteen. She didn't need to be thinking about that yet!

And so it was, on this quiet evening, that as the princess alighted from her horse and led him along the stone path outside the castle walls, she began to dream of her future. She stood still for a moment to kiss Victory's nose and to gaze at the distant mountains, which reminded her of the horizons that lay ahead in her life. The princess was enjoying these peaceful moments alone when her thoughts were unexpectedly interrupted by the low and soothing voice of the alligator swimming in the moat below the bridge on which she stood.

"Good evening to thee, fair princess," he began.

"Why, thank you, and a good evening to thee as well," she answered.

"What brings such a lovely young lady outside tonight?"

"Oh, I be just returning from a visit with my aunt and uncle, and I had a mind to capture a quick walk around the castle to enjoy the evening breeze."

"Alone?" the alligator questioned.

"I like to be alone. It gives me time to think and to pray."

"Oh, I see," he said slowly.

After a moment of silence the alligator continued, "May I ask what the princess enjoys thinking about when she is not interrupted by an annoyance such as myself?"

"My father tells me that my time is precious and must be used wisely. I was just considering how many things I hope to do in my life, how I can best serve the kingdom, and how I might be able to bring hope and joy to those who have none."

"My princess, thou art very ambitious and wise, but I fear thou art forgetting one minor point. You live in a castle. You live with your parents. You are sheltered. You have neither the knowledge nor the experience necessary to do the things of which you dream."

"My father says I do."

"Thy father is indeed a noble man, but dear Princess, he cannot possibly be right about everything. He loves you and therefore fears that harm may come to you if you are not constantly by his side. It is true he wants only your best, but Princess, I fear he is misguided. In the end, you are the one who will face the consequences of his unintentional yet serious mistakes."

"What are you saying I should do?"

"Nothing as of yet," replied the alligator. "But when the time comes, be ready to make your own decisions, or you will never survive in the real world."

Feeling a few sprinkles of raindrops on her arm and hearing the first roll of thunder, the princess took Victory to his stall and hurried inside.

Safeguards to Embrace

Most princesses like to think about romance—and I suspect that you are no exception. As a daughter of the King of Kings, your heavenly Father has only the very best in store for you. A true princess must not settle for anything less.

I have known many young ladies who were consumed with dating and thoughts about boyfriends, and thus wasted the years of their youth. I have seen many girls who had much potential for the Lord but who followed the typical way of most teenagers and missed out on God's best. On the other hand, I have had the joy of seeing the Lord bring together some outstanding couples and bless them with beautiful marriages. What made the difference?

The difference was not ultimately a result of how they met, how they got to know each other, or whether they called their relationship "dating," "courtship," "betrothal," or anything else. Rather, the difference was the result of decisions made long before—decisions to put Jesus first in every area of life, to stand alone for what was right, and to patiently follow God's way even when the road was uphill or difficult. The decisions we make in our youth play a huge role in determining our future.

Temptation in this area of boy/girl relationships is one of the biggest snares that the enemy uses to damage the lives and testimonies of Christian young people. Many lives have been destroyed. Many others have survived only with scars, pain, and heartache.

A true princess realizes this danger and understands her own need to be protected. This is not evidence of weakness or fear, but rather it is evidence of true courage. It requires courage to do things God's way, to wait for His timing, and to trust that He will bring you and your life partner together according to His perfect plan. It takes courage to obey when you do not understand.

For this reason, one of the wisest decisions you can make now is to embrace specific safeguards of protection. Notice that I say *embrace*. Many young ladies will *tolerate* what they consider to be "rules" or "laws" made by others. But tolerating them is not enough; you must make them your own. It is your *heart*—your own internal commitments before the Lord—that will make the difference. Only those who have formed their own personal convictions will have the strength required to remain pure and the discernment needed to escape temptation.

DESIRE THE BEST

As you are beginning this book, commit yourself to wanting God's *best* in your life—God's *best* in your future marriage. Maybe this seems obvious to you. Maybe you're thinking, "Of course I desire the best in my marriage." But when it comes right down to it, are you truly willing to make the required sacrifices and to wait for the best?

Since marriage is a picture of our relationship with Christ, God created marriage to be the most beautiful, joyful, and fulfilling earthly relationship we will ever experience. A good marriage is priceless. No one would want to trade it for anything—*or would they?* Countless young people are willing to forfeit the beautiful marriage God wants to give them in exchange for short-term thrills. If we could grasp how wonderful God's plan for us is, don't you think we'd be willing to wait? Don't you think we would purpose to enter into marriage pure rather than with emotional baggage and scars?

Think of your favorite storybook romance. You know, one where the couple lives happily ever after. Those fairy tales are just a joke, right? I mean no one actually has a marriage like that, do they? That is what Satan wants you to think—that there are no happy marriages. He doesn't want us to experience the blessings and the fulfilling marriage God wants to give. Even though all marriages have trials to work through, God's design is for them to be successful, fulfilling, and joyous. Jesus says, *"The thief cometh not, but for to steal, and to kill, and to destroy: I am come that they might have life, and that they might have it more abundantly"* (Jn. 10:10).

By observing the reckless way most young people live, you'd never know that deep down in their hearts they desire to one day have a wonderful marriage. They actually do desire a good marriage, but they've lost sight of this dream because they've already done so much to destroy it. In an effort to defend their actions, they will claim that such a marriage is idealistic or impossible, but in reality, they are simply unwilling to pay the price. It is too hard for them to wait—too hard to trust God.

Of course, your marriage will not actually be *perfect*. We live in a sinful world. But choose to *desire* the very best marriage, and refuse to lower your standard or settle for average. Many happy couples who faithfully prepared and waited can joyfully testify that God's blessings and rewards are more than worth the sacrifice.

To be rescued, one must first be a princess.

Now Is the Time to Prepare

"You know what, Sarah?" a fifteen-year-old friend told me recently. "It's really true. God's plans are so much better than we could ever imagine. My older brother is planning to be a pastor. He had such a long list of specific requirements for his future wife that our family used to tease him. We insisted that he'd never get married—that such a girl didn't exist. But then he met Lori! She is so perfect for him. She not only fits every one of his qualifications—she far surpasses them! It's incredible to see how God brought exactly the wife he needed. He wasn't willing to lower his standards, and God blessed his faith."

Stories like this are exciting. They remind me that our God is powerful, faithful, and concerned about every detail of our lives. Now obviously, if we truly desire God's best in our lives, then we need to be willing to marry *God's* choice. It's equally important to recognize that a happy marriage takes two people. If we desire a godly, loving husband, we need to do our part by preparing to be the best marriage partner that we can be. This starts today. Right now.

WHAT IS PURITY?

There are many young ladies who feel that because they have already made mistakes, purity is no longer possible for them. Therefore, it's important for all of us to understand that there are two kinds of purity.

First, there is the *innocent*, or *clean* type. Imagine a white cloth which has never been dirty or contaminated—it is pure. This idea of "innocence" might be the first thing that comes to our mind when we think of purity.

But there is a second kind of purity—the washed kind. Something was dirty, but it's been washed, it's been cleansed. A white rag may have been used to clean up a filthy mess, but once it has been thoroughly cleaned, it is pure and spotless again. It was black, but now it's white. *"Therefore if any man be in Christ, he is a new creature: old things are passed away; behold, all things are become new"* (II Cor. 5:17).

Of course, when it comes to our relationship with Christ (our salvation) we all have the "cleansed" type of purity. Proverbs 20:9 says, *"Who can say, I have made my heart clean, I am pure from my sin?"* The obvious answer is none of us. We are all guilty before God (Rom. 3:23). We all need to be cleansed and washed by the blood of Jesus. He makes us clean. He makes our hearts pure. He is able to turn filthy rags into pure white righteousness (Is. 1:18).

In light of this, it's important to realize that purity is offered to anyone—no matter what your past has been, no matter what mistakes you have made. As you are reading this book, the enemy may try to discourage you. Satan wants you to think it's too late to change. He wants you to feel hopeless and worthless. He wants you to give up. Do not believe his lies. It is never too late to turn to the Lord and experience the joy, peace, and abundant life He offers. If you begin to think that it is too late for you, then I encourage you to skip ahead to pages 194-198 and read the miraculous stories of what God can do through the life of one who is truly repentant. Regardless of how impossible it may seem to you, God is still calling you to purity, and not just to purity—to radiant purity!

WHAT IS RADIANT PURITY?

Well, I believe that *inward* purity is *outwardly* visible. It's seen in our countenance. It's seen in our eyes. It's seen by our joy. It's seen as we boldly take a stand—not just "going along" with this idea of purity, but excitedly making it known to others.

You see, radiant purity is much more than simply "innocence," it is the commitments, convictions, and attitudes that maintain innocence and that proclaim it to others. Believe me, radiant purity is noticed by the world, and it will lead others to follow the same path!

BEFORE YOU READ ANY MORE...

... I'd like to explain that as I write this book I'm assuming that you already agree with the following presuppositions. I want you to know where I'm coming from. If you don't, then you may be confused by some of the things I say.

1. The Bible is the inspired Word of God and should govern every area of our lives.
2. There is a problem with boy/girl relationships in our society. In this book I don't think it's necessary to go into detail about the sin and devastation happening in many lives around us, but I'm making the assumption that you agree there is a problem. The world's approach to relationships isn't working very well. Unhappy marriages, divorce, and broken, hurting families are not the way God intends things to be.
3. We want something different. I'm writing to young ladies who are seeking the Lord with all of their heart and who genuinely desire God's best. For this reason, I'm going to be courageous and honest as I share what I have observed and learned. Some

things that I encourage you to consider may not be easy, but because I believe you are sincerely longing for God's very best way, I have confidence that you are not afraid to take the narrow road, to stand for righteousness, and to put Jesus first—even when it's hard.

One last thing I need to tell you is that often in this book I am going to mention parents and the benefits that can come from our parents' help. I realize that many of you come from hurting families. Also, some of you have only one parent, and some of your parents may not be Christians. Do not let this discourage you or lead you to say, "Well, this can't work for me."

God has put you in exactly the family in which He wants you to be. He knows your parents' shortcomings, and He will not neglect you even for a moment. If you are seeking the Lord, He will faithfully supply the help you need (Phil. 4:19). When parents are not protecting or leading, He may choose to guide you through a wise older couple at your church or other godly mentors. Keep these things in mind as you continue reading.

Suggested Memory Verse:

"Let us be glad and rejoice, and give honor to Him: for the marriage of the Lamb is come, and His wife hath made herself ready" (Revelation 19:7).

Before You Meet Prince Charming

CHAPTER TWO

Dangers With the Dating System

*"This I say then, Walk in the Spirit, and ye
shall not fulfill the lust of the flesh."*
Galatians 5:16

The castle was a busy place, filled with music and laughter, banquets and feasts. The princess was loved by all. She was friends with many of the servants and guards, and she enjoyed meeting the many knights, ambassadors, and dignitaries who frequently reported to the king. The princess learned much from their intriguing stories, and she endeavored to make their time at the castle a lovely experience.

Even though these days were joyous and fruitful, the princess would occasionally find herself pondering the words of the alligator. She tried to dismiss his counsel as foolish, but sometimes it left questions in her mind, and once in a while it even began to sound attractive.

One day, while pondering these things, she decided to speak about the matter to her father.

"Permit me, my father, to ask of thee a question," she said courteously.

"Ask on, my daughter," he replied.

"May I go to the Spring Fair?"

"What be the purpose of thy request?"

"The alligator told me it be necessary that I socialize. He fears that I be sheltered."

"The walls of this castle were built not to confine but to protect," the king said. *"The wise need not live in a prison. Furthermore, thou surely knowest that stone walls are not able to sufficiently protect. A fair maiden must have inner walls in heart and mind. These are the greater protection."*

"Inner walls?" she asked.

"Yes, inner walls of conviction built out of the granite blocks of principle and wisdom from our heavenly Father."

"But is it true what the alligator says?" the princess repeated, pushing her hair behind her ear and looking up at him with questioning blue eyes. "Am I sheltered?"

"Thou art a candle—not to be hid under a bushel, but set on a candlestick," the king answered gently. "One who is pure in heart and life dost shine so brightly that others are confused by what they see. They say thou art sheltered, but such be not true. Thou art pure and clean, not because of the rules set by others, but by thine own choosing. Carefully then, guard thy heart and thy mind from evil. It matters not what others think."

"But what about the Spring Fair?" she persisted. "All the other maidens will be there, and they have asked me to join them."

"All the others? Surely, thou dost not seek their approval?"

"No, Father," she said slowly. "But if I never experience the real world, I fear that I will never fit in."

"Fit in?" he said in surprise. "Who saith anything about fitting in? Of course, thou wilt not fit in. Dost thou wish to be like the other maidens and youth?"

"Oh no! They are silly and chase after vain things," she answered. "But Father, what thinkest thou of the alligator's words? Do you not think that I should socialize?"

"It depends on thy purpose," he answered.

"The alligator says I will never meet a prince if I do not learn to mingle more freely as do others," the princess sighed. "He says the other maidens socialize oft with the young men in the village."

"But you say you do not wish to be like the other maidens. And besides, such is not befitting a princess. My daughter, thy role is not to fit into the world—but to change it. You are called to give light to a world of darkness. Indeed, thou art already a light. Thanks be to God that thou art a candle, and though thou be young, yet thou art a bright one!"

"But are you not overly cautious?" she asked. The princess thought her father looked very wise with his full, dark beard and his blue eyes that were so deep and pure. Yet, even though she knew deep down that his counsel was right, his words seemed hard to accept.

"Dear Princess," he responded, "few treasures are so easily lost as thy purity—yet few so important to keep."

The princess was quiet for a moment as she thought on these things. Then she proceeded, slowly trying to find the right words for her questions. "Father, what do you mean by—?"

But the king interrupted her. "Follow me," he said with the hint of a smile. "I want to show you something."

"Very well," she agreed. "Are we going to the village?"

"No, to the flower garden."

The princess followed her father through the palace, past rows of strong pillars, under a high overhanging roof, and through a stone archway. They entered the sunlit garden of the back courtyard, which was well groomed, covered by a blue sky, and framed by beautiful

trees. Through the branches she could see the vine-covered walls of protection her father, grandfather, and forefathers had built, as well as the towers for the sentries who were ever guarding the castle. On both sides of the back courtyard were large, black, iron gates—strong and secure, but never closed except at night or during war. The king wished all of his subjects to visit his gardens, to enjoy them, and to learn from them.

"Look at this. What do you see?" her father questioned.

"A lovely rose," she said.

"What color?"

"White."

"Pure white," her father emphasized. "What else do you notice?"

"Well, it is closed. It is just a bud."

"What is the inside like?" he inquired. "Open it for me."

"I can't open it for you!"

"Why not?" he asked.

"Because it has to open by itself," she stated.

"But I want to see the inside," repeated the king.

"Then you will have to wait for it to open when it is ready. If I force it open, you will never see its beauty."

"But are you not overly cautious?" teased the king. "We'll only open a few petals."

"The rose is very delicate," she answered. "The petals will tear, and it will never be the same."

"And so it is with many fair maidens," the king explained. "Their beauty is never fully seen, for they wait not until the proper time. They are handled and played with by too many a fellow. Their heart is opened prematurely. The fragrance and beauty that was intended for the perfect time is lost or damaged forever."

"Yes, I understand now, Father," said the princess, "but all I want to do is go to the fair. I won't—"

"Thou mayest go to the fair if thou think it to be profitable, but first thou must understand how easily a heart can be stolen. Thou must purpose to be a white and pure rose—a bud that is still closed and one that will not give away the key to her heart until the time be right."

"How will I know the right time?"

"Thou wilt know. But it will not be for a while. Devote thyself to the business of thy heavenly Father. Learn to lay down thy life for others. In so doing, thou wilt be prepared for the noblest and bravest of knights, and no rose will be sweeter nor more beautiful than thee."

The American System

In the years preceding marriage, most Americans do something they call dating. This is actually a new thing—it is not the process that has been used throughout most of history. It is easy to allow ourselves to become comfortable with a system simply because we have grown up with it and are familiar with it. This is dangerous. Our thinking should be shaped by Scripture, not just current trends. After all, God's way is seldom the popular way. Too many rely on culture instead of the Word of God. Most people cannot even give solid answers for why they do what they do. They are simply following the crowd. Yet it is the Bible that is the standard by which we must evaluate every area of our lives.

If you look at the fruit of the American system of dating, there is reason to be seriously concerned. The majority of modern marriages end up in divorce. Few marriages are truly happy. And many enter into marriage with injuries, emotional handicaps, and scars from past dating relationships.

MARRY A CHRISTIAN

"Hi! I'm Sarah. What's your name?" I asked the girl next to me as I arrived at a friend's home, found a comfortable chair, and began getting acquainted with some people I didn't know. It turned out that this young lady who seemed to be a nice Christian girl was just about my age. After a few minutes of small talk, she told me her big news— she was getting married soon.

"That's exciting! How did you meet him?" I asked.

As she began to tell her story, I started to feel a little uneasy.

"So does he go to the same church as you?" I asked.

"Well, no, he's not really 'into church'—but I'm hoping that will change."

She said this as if it were no big deal. I was shocked! She was about to marry a man who wasn't even a Christian, and she didn't seem to care. Didn't she realize what she was doing?

The answer is that, whether she realized it or not, she was unable to exercise discernment and make a logical decision because she was already attached. She couldn't dream of *not* marrying him now. In fact, she told me that since they had started dating (six months earlier) they had never been apart for more than about twenty-four hours. "I haven't seen him since yesterday," she sighed. "I feel like I'm going through withdrawal."

Sadly, this young lady is not the only Christian girl who is being led astray by marrying a nonbeliever. This crisis is happening all around us. I expect that you personally know of some couples in which one spouse is a believer and the other is not. Why does this happen? The Bible is clear that Christians should marry only Christians (I Cor. 7:39, II Cor. 6:14). So why do we see so many believers marrying unbelievers? How could this be happening?

We could make a list of possible reasons:

1. It could be that one of them lied. You know, a guy will say anything for a girl, and vice versa.
2. Perhaps one of them was sincerely deceived and considered himself to be a believer, but didn't understand the gospel—that Christianity is a personal relationship with Jesus Christ, formed at the moment in time when one specifically and genuinely asks Christ for forgiveness and mercy.
3. Maybe they both went to the same church or were from the same denomination and therefore just assumed that the other was a Christian.
4. They might have believed that after marriage they would be able to lead their spouse to the Lord.
5. Possibly, they felt pressured into getting married by circumstances or other people.

6. Maybe one of them got saved after they were married. Well, that's a good problem! Someone came to know the Lord.

We could continue to list other possible scenarios, but actually there is just **one main reason** for unbalanced marriages—it's called dating!

Here's how it happens: Jared invites Jessica on a date. Jessica doesn't think Jared is a Christian, but she agrees to go because, after all, it's only a date! They go out together and have a really nice time. Jessica thinks Jared is so funny! And Jared finds Jessica to be very insightful and considerate. They go out together again and have a great talk—in fact, Jessica says it's one of the best talks she's ever had with a guy. The two of them start to get close. You see, dating is a very emotional thing. Bonds are formed quickly. Before Jessica even realizes what has happened, she and Jared are attached. They've become best friends. They share everything. Soon affection enters the picture. The bonds she had intended to form with her future life partner, she has now formed prematurely with someone who isn't even a Christian and who definitely doesn't have the traits she was looking for in a husband. But how can she break up now? It would be too painful. Jessica easily justifies the relationship (because after all, they love each other, and that's all that matters—right?), and they get married.

One of the problems is that even though nearly everybody has high standards for the one whom they will one day marry, they don't uphold those same high standards when they date. "It's only a date," they say, not realizing the emotional bonds that form so quickly and easily. Then they often experience deep pain by breaking up, or they marry someone who is lacking in spiritual strength or maybe isn't even a Christian at all.

Have the Right Perspective

Someone might argue, "Yes, I see that dating a non-believer is definitely foolish, but if we will just be careful to date strong Christians, everything will be okay, right?" Well, I'm afraid not. There are some more dangers with the dating system in general:

- People date in order to have a good time right now. Many times they're not actually planning to get married. This is a crucial point: *they are not planning long-term commitment.* But why date and get attached to someone who is not going to be your life partner? Dating is thinking about fun now rather than loyalty to your one lifelong partner and the joy of the best marriage later. *In other words, the world's way is "**now oriented.**" God's way is "**future oriented.**"*

- Most young people plan to date a number of different individuals in order to get to know a variety of people—and then pick the best one to marry. What they fail to realize is that the process that forms bonds begins with the very first relationship. Then the break-up process is very painful. *In other words, the world's way involves the **pain of separation**. God's way involves **no separation**.*

- Much of the dating we see today is "me oriented" (to bring *me* security, enjoyment, fulfillment, etc.) and often leaves hurt and pain in the lives of others. True love always puts others first and focuses on their needs. *In other words, the world's way is to **get**. God's way is always to **give**.*

- People start dating long before they are considering marriage. Just think of all the "dating" that happens even in elementary or middle school. Boys and girls "date" because it's a thrill or a tempting experiment—not because they are committed to this person. *In other words, the world's way is for **pleasure**. God's way is for **commitment**.*

- The Bible does not give any positive examples of anything even close to dating. In our modern world, everyone is comfortable with the dating system simply because it's what everyone does. *In other words, the world's way is built on **human thinking, tradition, and culture**. God's way is always based on the **Word of God**—Biblical standards, principles, and goals.*

- People date, planning to break up if things don't work out. This seems like practice for divorce, not marriage! *In other words, the world's way is **temporary**. God's way is **permanent**.*

A good way to sum up this list would be to say that dating, as we know it in America, tends to follow the **patterns of the flesh** (our earthly self which is weak and naturally sinful). But our goal is to follow God's way—the **pattern of the Spirit.** This rivalry between the flesh and the Spirit is a basic theme that is evident throughout Scripture. The flesh seeks to control, but it is the Spirit that must dominate. Dating is a good example of this rivalry.

"This I say then, Walk in the Spirit, and ye shall not fulfill the lust of the flesh. For the flesh lusteth against the Spirit, and the Spirit against the flesh: and these are contrary the one to the other: so that ye cannot do the things that ye would" (Gal. 5:16–17).

Thou shalt not build thy castle on sand.

What Is God's Way?

So what is the alternative? How will we ever get married if we don't date? Well, God doesn't give us ten easy steps to finding the right life partner. Instead, Scripture is filled with principles and concepts that teach us what we need to know in order to make wise decisions.

The specific way God brings people together will be different in every case. But we can trust that as we choose to flee from the patterns of the flesh, to walk in the Spirit, and to apply God's principles in our lives, God will lead us to our future life partner in His way and at the perfect time. In the rest of this book, we will be reviewing how to seek God's ways and avoid the thinking of the world.

PAIRING OFF AND BREAKING UP

"Oh brother," I said to myself, as I glanced at my friend's folder and noticed that in big letters she had written, "Call Tony tonight!!!" She was only ten years old, yet it appeared as if her whole world revolved around her boyfriends. They seemed to give her security, and she wanted our whole class at school to know who she was "going with." I was in a Christian school only up through fifth grade (and then started homeschooling), but I remember that even in elementary school the juiciest news was always "who likes who." Various friends seemed to continually be pairing off, breaking up, choosing a new boyfriend, breaking up again, and so on.

I am extremely grateful that I was blessed with parents who protected me, helped me to see the dangers of the dating system when I was still young, and gave me a vision for something better. Yet, even though I had made the decision that I didn't want to follow the world's system of dating, I often found myself around girls who didn't have quite the same ideas as I had. When I was thirteen, I spent several days at a Christian event for youth. I guess I shouldn't have been surprised that a lot of the young people seemed more interested in flirting than they were in the Word of God. As I walked through the halls, I kept overhearing snickering and gossip.

"Did you hear that Regina broke up with Josh? She's going with Alex now," one girl commented.

"Really?" the other would squeal. "Well, did you hear about Susie and Jonathan?"

Everyone seemed to be walking around in pairs, hanging on each other, and spreading the latest news. I knew it was distracting me, but it seemed impossible to avoid. The subject of guys just kept coming up. One afternoon about six friends and I were sitting around, munching on snacks and chatting about the events of the weekend. In the midst of our conversation, an eleven-year-old girl in the group lowered her voice a little and said, "You guys, I've **got** to tell you something. Don't tell anyone this because I know it sounds crazy ... but ... I think Kevin likes me. I know he's a lot older than I am, but he's been staring at me all week!" It seemed as if dating consumed everyone's thoughts and conversations. I began to wonder if girls could make it even ten minutes without bringing up a comment about which guy they liked or who they thought liked them.

All this dating seemed foolish to me at the time, but looking back on it now, it seems even more silly. And not just silly—*dangerous*. It was almost like a big game: Date. Have fun. Break up. Date someone else. Have fun. Break up. None of these kids were considering marriage, so what was the goal of their dating? In Scripture, we do not see any examples of couples pursuing romantic relationships except for the purpose of marriage. I would assume that most of the friends I met at this Christian event thirteen years ago are now married. Do you think their dating experiences over the three-day event are benefiting their marriages today?

As I watched this pattern of pairing off and breaking up with different individuals at my Christian school, in extracurricular activities, and at church, I remember thinking that in our family we were going to do things differently. I had no idea how God might one day bring me a husband or what I would end up doing with my life, but I knew at least two things:

1. I wanted to wait for God to bring the right person.
2. When it was the right time, I knew that I wanted my parents to be involved. I figured that we would be a team working on this together.

That was all I needed to know. Actually, that is still all I need to know. I don't know if or when I'll get married or how God will bring it about, but up to this point, He has made it clear to me that right now He has work for me to do as a single woman. I don't have to date, flirt, or be searching for a husband. The Lord is more than able to arrange my marriage without my help. So in that sense, one could say that I believe in "arranged marriages." But you see, God is the One doing the arranging. Can you imagine anything better than a couple who is just right for each other coming together in exactly the right way at the right time? Only God can bring about something so perfect.

BUT HOW WILL I GET TO KNOW SOMEONE?

You probably are acquainted with dozens of boys whom you are sure that you would never marry. And do you know what? You didn't have to date them to find that out!

I'm sure that there are many people whom you know well even though you haven't dated them. You will form friendships with people just by observing them at church, family get-togethers, school activities, or by working with them in ministry opportunities. Actually, you will really get to know a young man better this way. You can see what he is truly like and how he responds in various real life situations—not just in a romantic relationship.

When God brings the right one into your life, He'll give you opportunities to get to know him. The specifics as to how this happens will be different in every situation. Parents can often provide lots of help and advice. But it is essential to remember that there is no reason to cultivate a romantic relationship for any other purpose than the objective of marriage.

SUGGESTED MEMORY VERSE:

"This I say then, Walk in the Spirit, and ye shall not fulfill the lust of the flesh" (Galatians 5:16).

SUGGESTED ASSIGNMENT:

A young lady once wrote me a letter saying how hard it was for her because she didn't have anyone to date. This hurting girl was lonely and frustrated, and she kept noticing everyone else with their boyfriends. She was feeling so desperate that she began writing letters to guys she knew, inviting them to events, and trying to get their attention. If this girl asked you for advice, what would you tell her? What suggestions would you give her? Write a sample letter, giving some counsel to this young lady. Be sure you include Scripture in your answer.

*If thou winnest her hand,
thou must marry her.*

Consequences of Dating

TESTIMONY FROM A YOUNG LADY

When I was about fourteen years old, my dad had a talk with me about the dangers of dating. His cautions made a lot of sense to me, and I made the decision to wait on God's timing rather than focus on boys and dating. As I got older, however, I found that it is one thing to *say* I have a commitment, but it is *another* thing to truly have a conviction in my heart.

My life did not match up with what I said I believed. I had a wrong attitude about guys, and I constantly seemed to be desiring attention from young men. One time when I noticed a guy looking at me and giving me a lot of attention, I foolishly chose to accept it, and soon I began seeking for more. Before I knew it, I was also flirting with him, looking for ways to be with him, and giving him "pieces of my heart." I knew he wasn't the right one for me, but I encouraged him simply because I enjoyed the attention. I wasn't thinking about the consequences.

Another time I began to e-mail a young man who liked me, even though I knew my parents did not approve. I knew I'd never marry him, but I was enjoying the "fun" relationship, not thinking about my future marriage. One compromise led to another, and I ended up disobeying my parents by dating a couple of guys along the way. I knew this wasn't God's best, but since my heart wasn't right, I easily gave in to temptation. I wanted to change, and I kept confessing things to my parents and to the Lord, but it seemed that I just kept making the same mistakes over and over again.

Then one day a godly young man approached my father saying he would like to get to know me better. I couldn't believe it! He was the kind of man I had always dreamed of marrying. I wanted to give him my whole heart, and it was hard confessing my past relationships. As we sought the Lord's will for our lives, we saw Him bring us together in a wonderful way. By God's grace, we saved our first kiss for our wedding. We are truly grateful to God for how He has blessed our marriage.

From the perspective of someone who is now married, I urge you to prepare yourselves for marriage by waiting for your future mate. The relationships I had with young men before I was married were not profitable, but hurtful. I was not thinking of my future marriage at the time. It is difficult for both my husband and I to completely forget the past feelings and affections we gave others.

Don't deceive yourself by believing that the decisions you make now won't affect your future. Premature romantic relationships *will* cause heartache later. I am happy to say that we serve a gracious and merciful God who gives us so much more than we deserve. In spite of past mistakes, the Lord is able to give true healing and genuine joy. He heals and restores. But this doesn't mean that there won't be consequences or scars. My husband and I rejoice to see the wonderful things the Lord continues to do in our lives. Psalm 23:3 says, *"He restoreth my soul: He leadeth me in the paths of righteousness for His name's sake."*

CHAPTER THREE

Guard Your Heart

*"Keep [guard] thy heart with all diligence; for out
of it are the issues [wellspring] of life."*
Proverbs 4:23

After much thought and several more talks with her parents, the princess decided to go to the Spring Fair. However, she knew why she was going—not to get, but to give. Not to make friends, but to be a friend. Not to fit into the crowd, but to demonstrate to others an example of true royalty.

"Good-bye, Father. Farewell, Mother," the princess said excitedly on the morning of the fair. "Thank you again for your helpful advice."

She fed Victory an apple, mounted him gracefully, and enthusiastically began her journey. Victory seemed excited today too.

The princess wondered what new experiences the day might hold. As she was riding across the bridge just outside the castle, she was stopped by a voice.

"Where, fair Princess, art thou headed this fine day?" began the alligator.

"I'm going to the Spring Fair, and I be in a hurry. I have not the time to speak with thee now," she answered, squinting in the bright sunlight.

"Well then, have a splendid day. It is a good thing that thou art headed to the fair. Thou wilt like it. I am glad that thou hast finally begun to make thine own decisions."

"Thou art mistaken, sir," she replied, as she turned Victory to face the moat, "for I have always made my own decisions—as does everyone else. Some make wise ones, and others make foolish ones. Some listen to wise counsel, and others reject it. But each person decides for himself which course he will take."

"But some are so hidden in their own little world that they do not know what is happening in the world around them," objected the alligator. "True, there is evil in the world. But you must get used to it, or in the end thou wilt be most dreadfully shocked."

"I can think of no more dangerous position than to learn to tolerate evil in order to become accustomed to reality," the princess said

boldly. "The one who becomes comfortable with that which is corrupt is quick to accept it, and what one accepts, he will soon embrace. I pray that I will always be shocked by the evil of the 'real world.' "

"You misunderstand me," replied the alligator. "I only intend to suggest that you learn to be independent. Thou wilt gain from new experiences, and it will be healthy for thee to socialize with friends of thine own age."

"I have not time to argue. However, your foolish words only make the words of my father to seem yet wiser. Let me just say that the one who socializes merely for his own purposes is foolish. And now, I must be going."

Anxious to be on her way, the princess rode quickly down the stone road. Soon she could hear voices and music coming from the fair. Remembering what her father had said about how she must have inner walls of protection, the princess purposed to be a white and pure rose closed until the right time, as well as a bright candle giving light to others.

Upon her arrival, she entrusted Victory to the town stable and began to mingle with the young ladies chatting in the park. The princess made friends quickly. She never acted as if she believed she ought to be treated as royalty. Rather, she was quick to serve, to fellowship with the villagers, and to put others first. Her kind words, gracious manners, and loving actions were obvious to all. In fact, if she had taken note, she would have realized that she received much more respect and honor as a result of these humble actions than she ever would have gained had she demanded admiration from others or proclaimed her own importance. But she did not even notice what others thought of her, for, as I said before, she was a true princess.

Around noon, she seated herself on a blanket in the middle of the park, joining a company of her girlfriends who were about to set out a picnic. Just then she heard a pleasant voice behind her. Turning around, she found herself looking into the cheerful face of one of the young knights.

"Princess, why sit ye here among the youth? One so honorable as thyself deserves a seat of dignity. Please join me at the table over yonder. I would much appreciate thy fellowship."

"Why, thank you," the princess replied, but with a little hesitation continued, "I really am just fine here. I enjoy the children and have met several lovely village girls."

"Oh, Princess, please come join me," he entreated.

"I'm honored by your request, but really, I'd prefer to stay here."

"Naturally. You ought to stay. Thy humility and kindness put me to shame. Of course the young ladies will appreciate thy friendship. But may I join thee here?" he asked.

"Um, well, certainly."

"My name is Sir Eloquence," he said loudly as he immediately sat down right beside her and began conversing freely. "Tell me about the castle and thy plans for the future. I have long been a friend of thy family."

The princess wondered why she had never heard of him if he had been a friend for so long. She soon began to think that she had been too quick to welcome his company. Nevertheless, she answered his questions graciously and spoke of her family and their concerns for the kingdom. The young knight listened attentively to the princess's every word, laughed at her stories, and told many interesting tales himself. She enjoyed his fellowship, but she was also beginning to feel uncomfortable by his overly friendly manner.

"May I accompany you home?" Sir Eloquence asked.

"Thank you, but I prefer to ride alone. It was nice to meet you, though," she said. Then, without giving him time to respond, she added, "Good-bye! I enjoyed our visit."

All the way home the princess pondered the events of the day. "Was I too friendly with Sir Eloquence? What if he is the right one? How do I know if I am guarding my heart?"

The wise princess knew exactly whom she should ask for advice!

How Do I Protect My Heart?

The heart is more than just emotions. It is the internal driving force of everything we do. What the heart desires is the most powerful force in our lives. Therefore, we need to make sure to guard it from those influences that would seek to divert, pollute, or steal our hearts.

First, let's think about the practical ways to guard our heart as we interact with young men. In the previous chapter we discussed the dangers of the dating system. Choosing not to date gives us a whole new freedom in relationships, yet we still have to figure out how we are going to respond to the young men we meet in our everyday lives.

Guys do lots of dumb and immature things to get girls' attention (and vice versa). My mom told me that when she was in college, guys used to shoot peas at girls during lunch. Using their spoon as a catapult, they would send peas through the cafeteria and onto a table where some girls were trying to enjoy their meal. Probably not the best way to introduce themselves!

When I was in second grade and attending a Christian school, my girlfriends informed me that a boy in my class named Chad had a crush on me and wanted to kiss me. I was not very excited to hear the news. But it definitely caught me by surprise when at recess some of Chad's friends told him they would help catch me. Then the race began—all around the playground. I'm not sure why I didn't just run to the teacher, but instead I ran around the slide, around the merry-go-round, around the slide again, inside the jungle gym—and that's when I got caught ... and kissed ... on my cheek. I thought it was very unpleasant, but at least now that he had accomplished his mission, he seemed to forget about his crush.

Throughout our lives, we will obviously encounter all sorts of young men. We need to know how to respond. We need to know how to form friendships while still guarding our hearts. We need to know when to flee. You probably won't encounter a guy chasing you around a playground tomorrow, but let's say you are sitting in church and a nice-looking young man walks up to you and begins a conversation. How should you respond? Or perhaps you are involved in a ministry in which you work with both guys and girls. How friendly should you be with the young men? What if a guy starts following you around?

RESPONDING WISELY TO BOYS

Feeling confused and a little distressed, my sister Grace cornered my brother Stephen, saying, "Pleeeease help! This guy keeps following me around and talking to me. It's getting really annoying, and I don't know what to do!" This friendly young man at the conference we were attending kept hanging around our family and talking to Grace, who was fourteen years old at the time. At first Grace just tried to be friendly, but after a few hours of being followed, she was getting rather frustrated. Grace tried everything. She ignored him, but he didn't seem to get the point. Then she sat down and started to read, but he just came right up to her and started a conversation. Grace asked Stephen to try to distract him, but the young man didn't seem too interested in talking with Stephen. She tried walking around. But whenever she stopped—guess who was right behind her? He was a polite, friendly guy who just wanted to be friends, but it was driving Grace nuts.

As we were cleaning up from the conference late in the afternoon, I walked into a dark classroom where one of the sessions had been held to collect a few items. I flipped on the light and was startled to find someone in the room! It was Grace. She was hiding in the dark so that this "special friend" wouldn't be able to find her!

Okay, hiding in the dark or racing around the playground is probably not the best way to deal with guys who like you. But what should you do? Many girls struggle with knowing the right way to respond in these situations.

Once as I was standing in a church, I noticed a group of girls hesitantly walking toward me. Observing their sheepish smiles and muffled snickering, I figured that they had something they wanted to ask.

"We have a question," one of them finally said. "I was wondering what you think about, well, do you think it's okay, um, I guess, what I mean is, uh, I have a lot of *friends* who are *boys* … I like to hang out with them … is that okay?"

I've been asked similar questions many times. Girls ask,

"Is it okay to write or e-mail boys?"

"How should I respond to a young man who is friendly with me?"

"I'm a tomboy. What if I like to be with boys more than girls?"

"What should I say to friends who are always talking about guys?"

Good questions. Let's discuss them. It really comes down to this:

how do we guard our hearts? First of all, yes, of course it is okay to be friends with young men. Obviously, it is important to be cheerful, polite, and friendly. Christian young men are our brothers in Christ and should be treated as such. At the same time, there are some important cautions to keep in mind.

1. KEEP THE FRIENDSHIP CASUAL.

There are different levels of friendships: acquaintances, casual friendships, close friendships, and intimate friendships.

In order to save your heart for one and not give it away to the wrong person, friendships with young men need to stay at the acquaintance or casual level. It doesn't take long for a relationship with a guy to move from a casual friendship to something more than that. Sometimes you as a young lady may not even realize what is happening, but soon you find that bonds have formed and you are emotionally attached to a young man whom you only intended to have as a casual friend.

One way to guard your heart is to be careful not to share personal or intimate things with your guy friends. It is great to encourage each other in the Lord and share how the Lord is working in your life, but if you open up and share your heart with him, you will most likely become too attached. In most situations, it is better to try to keep conversations short. Be aware of the fact that it is easy to give away a piece of your heart to a young man without dating him at all. During this time in your life, focus on becoming best friends with your family members and building relationships with godly young ladies. Remember, the point isn't to avoid guys, but to protect and guard your heart from being given away prematurely. Emotional intimacy belongs to your spouse.

2. AVOID SITUATIONS THAT WILL BREED EMOTIONAL BONDS.

Don't spend time alone with one young man or single one out in a group. When you are at church, school, or other events, it is good to stay in the company of several people or in families. If you get into a long one-on-one talk with a boy, you are putting yourself in a situation that can easily cause you to open up, connect with him, and find yourself in a more-than-casual friendship. It may mean nothing to him as a young man, but to you as a young lady, it will be a distraction and an emotional tie. The same thing applies to letter writing. I've had several young men ask me if they could write to me or e-mail me, and I have always explained to them that I'd rather not. I want to avoid deep friendships with guys until the right one comes along. It's our desire to be close eventually with *one*, but not with *many* in the meantime. Sure, I answer e-mails from guys who have something they need to ask me, and sometimes correspondence is necessary. But I have chosen to avoid any serious letter writing to young men.

Once premature, close friendships are formed, it's much harder to stay emotionally pure and focused on the Lord. I'm not trying to give you a list of rules, but I do want to emphasize the point that we as young ladies must guard our hearts diligently! Our natural tendency is to want to give our hearts away. In fact, God designed us to give our hearts away—but only to our future mate! If you show caution now by avoiding certain situations, you will avoid problems later. Proverbs 22:5 says, *"Thorns and snares are in the way of the froward: he that doth keep his soul shall be far from them."*

3. DON'T SEEK ATTENTION FOR YOURSELF.

Joe and Emily met at church. Even though he liked her right away, she did not think he could ever be the right one for her. Yet, since they saw each other every Sunday at church, they began to develop a friendship. Emily appreciated the attention he gave her. She was feeling a lack of approval and praise from her father, and so it was easy for her to look to Joe to meet her emotional needs. "We're only friends—nothing more," Emily told herself over and over again. "I don't need to worry about this. We aren't dating or anything." Soon they began to talk on the phone and to send e-mails and text messages. Emily told herself and everyone else that she wasn't interested in him, but Joe was falling in love with her. One day at church, he told her that he loved her. Immediately, she realized that her actions had been selfish. As she was soaking up the attention and justifying the friendship (which she never intended to be anything more than casual), she had actually been hurting him.

This is a common mistake we as young ladies can easily make—encouraging guys to be interested in us simply because we appreciate the attention. Yes, of course we naturally enjoy this kind of attention. It's fun. It feels good. But think about it—it's purely selfish. It easily hinders and distracts young men in their spiritual lives and breeds desires that cannot be fulfilled right now. It is called defrauding—taking something that doesn't belong to us. As girls, we can defraud by dressing in a way so that boys will notice us, flirting with our eyes, or even just by the way we smile at a certain time or laugh at every joke. You know what I mean. All these things communicate a message. Yes, we might get some of the attention we are looking for, but is it worth it? Is it godly? Is it the right way to treat our brothers in Christ?

4. ASK YOUR PARENTS FOR SPECIFIC GUIDANCE.

No two stories are ever exactly the same. Stories are different because people are different. Some people are naturally outgoing. Others tend to be quiet. Some are in public school. Others are homeschooled. Some go to college. Others stay at home. Some are acquainted with numerous godly young men. Others know only a few or maybe none at all.

The point is that every one of us is in a unique situation. We all have varying strengths and weaknesses. Fortunately, God, who knows our individual needs, has given each of us some special help tailored just for us—our parents! If you aren't sure how friendly to be with guys, ask your parents for advice. If you're worried that a guy likes you and you don't know how to respond, discuss the situation with your parents. Since our family members know us and understand our strengths and weaknesses, God can use them to give wise guidance.

A young man once visited our church. He was a newcomer and I wanted to be friendly, so I talked to him for a few minutes. I wasn't interested in him; I was just trying to be nice. Later that day we had an all-church dinner, and somehow I ended up next to him in line, so we talked some more. At lunch, I also found myself at the same table with this young man, so again we continued our discussion. After church, I remember thinking to myself, "I probably came across as way too friendly. I hope I didn't give the wrong impression. I need to be more careful."

The next time this young man visited our church, I sort of tried to avoid him and didn't talk to him at all. After church my mom came up to me and said, "Sarah, don't you think you could be a little more friendly with 'so and so'? You walked right past him today and didn't even look at him. You could have at least said hi."

The first time he visited I didn't mean to be overly friendly, and the second time I didn't intend to be rude. But it's easy to swing from one extreme to the other and end up being too friendly, too shy, or paranoid about talking to boys at all.

Discussing specific situations with my parents is what has helped me the most. They are able to discern how I am coming across to others and give wise counsel. Also, remember that if we stay focused on *giving* and simply doing what is right with pure motives, then we really don't need to fear what guys or anyone else may think of our actions. The less we think about ourselves, the better we are able to be gentle, sensitive, and guarded with men.

5. GUARD YOUR WORDS WHEN YOU ARE WITH FRIENDS.

"I think Ryan is so cute," I overheard my friend say.

"Yeah, I think so too. What do you think of Nick?" another friend asked.

"I'm trying to be more aggressive in getting to know guys," the first girl added.

Then they noticed me standing nearby.

"What do you think about this, Sarah?" they asked.

I didn't know what to say. I was about fifteen years old, and I didn't think this sounded like a very good conversation topic. I should have simply explained to them why I wanted to avoid this kind of discussion, but unfortunately I wasn't bold enough to be straightforward and tell them the truth. Instead, I simply avoided the question. Later I realized that I had missed an opportunity to share with these girls what the Lord had been teaching me about guarding our hearts. These young ladies had a wrong attitude regarding guys, and in the years that followed, this wrong perspective led to problems. I'm very sorry to say that both of these girls have made serious mistakes, and one of them is now divorced. I wonder if things might have turned out differently if I had been courageous enough to speak up when I had the chance?

These two girls were only about twelve and thirteen years old at the time—not nearly old enough to be thinking about marriage. They may not have been dating, but they already had a wrong attitude … a wrong perspective … wrong goals … and were following a wrong system. They were anxious to flirt with, get attention from, and develop relationships with guys. This dangerous outlook damages many young ladies.

This attitude is often encouraged and cultivated by our conversations with friends. Young ladies get together and look through magazines to pick out the cutest guys, talk about "who likes who," pass on gossip about the latest "couples," and discuss their favorite romance stories from movies they've seen recently. If you've been in a situation like this, I'm sure you agree that it is distracting! You want to focus on the Lord, but with everyone talking about boys all the time, you begin to wonder if it's even possible to control your thoughts. Not only do these useless conversations lead our thoughts in a wrong direction, but they breed discontentment and begin to make us feel that we are the "only girl" in the whole world without a boyfriend.

In an effort to guard your heart, choose friends who will edify you spiritually and build you up. If you find yourself surrounded by girls who are boy-crazy, be willing to stand alone by explaining to your friends why you are cautious about talking about boyfriends. Use these awkward situations as opportunities to teach others why they need to embrace some of the safeguards that you have chosen.

6. AVOID INFLUENCES THAT POLLUTE YOUR THOUGHTS.

If you truly desire to guard your heart, then it should be obvious to you that you ought to avoid any influences that distract your thoughts or stir up wrong desires. We've already talked about friends, but let's list a few others:

- **Movies and television**

  I'm sure you will agree that television is full of evil concepts, words, actions, and pictures that can quickly pollute our minds with worldly thinking. Watching TV is like dating the world. Television also tempts us to waste much valuable time. David says, *"I will set no wicked thing before mine eyes...."* *"Turn away mine eyes from beholding vanity..."* (Ps. 101:3, 119:37). Evaluate what you watch. How is it affecting your thoughts?

When I was eleven years old, my parents decided that the television was too hard to control, so they made the radical decision to actually remove it from our home. My friends asked me, "Sarah, how are you ever going to survive without a TV?" But I can honestly say that no one in our family has ever once regretted my parents' decision.

- **The Internet**

  All of the efforts and sacrifices our parents have made to protect us from the corruption of the world can be destroyed in a few moments of exposure to the thousands of evil things on the Internet. Be vigilant to guard your eyes. Make sure you have a protected Internet service. Be very careful about whom you get to know online, or about visiting chat rooms. Purpose to be accountable to your parents. Be sure to tell them if you run into something you didn't intend to see.

- **Music**

  I believe that Satan is using music in powerful ways to damage and pollute Christians today. Not only the words, but also the attitudes, moral bankruptcy of the songs, character of the musicians, and the addictive, physical drive of the beat all combine to create a rebellious, independent spirit which leads to dangerous, immoral patterns in young listeners.

  Examine the *source* of the music you listen to. Is it of the world? (See I John 2:15-16 and James 4:4.) Test the *fruit* of your music. Godly music must be edifying. Does the music focus the listener on the Lord? Just as wrong music pollutes our soul, so godly, melodious music uplifts and edifies our soul.

- **Books and magazines**

What kinds of books or magazines are you choosing to read? Ask the Lord to give you discernment, and remember that the enemy wants to use things that appear "good" to keep us from the "best." I especially want to warn you to be careful about romance novels—even Christian ones. They may seem innocent, yet they fill our minds with romance, causing us to dream in unrealistic ways about our future rather than delighting in Christ.

A well-meaning lady had a series of Christian books that she didn't need any more. She decided to give them as a gift to Alana, a twelve-year-old friend of mine. Alana was excited to start reading them right away, and she found them very interesting and enjoyable. For the most part, they were good, wholesome books teaching godly morals and Christian character. But there was one problem. All through the books were romantic stories of girls who fell in love and lived happily ever after. Soon Alana began to struggle with her thoughts. Throughout the day she would find herself fantasizing about her future and dreaming of the day when Prince Charming would come, sweep her off her feet, and marry her. Alana felt frustrated. After all, she was only twelve years old; she knew she didn't need to be thinking about that yet! As Alana discussed her struggle with her mother, the two of them decided that the first way to deal with these thoughts was to get rid of those books.

Recently, Alana told me how glad she is that she stopped reading them when she did. Many other girls have shared similar testimonies with me. As a daughter of the King of Kings, purpose to fill your mind with only the best—with what is pure, good, clean, and edifying. Proverbs 4:23 exhorts us to, *"Keep thy heart with all diligence; for out of it are the issues of life."* This means that we need to be very careful to protect ourselves from the influences that mold the interests of our heart, because our heart is going to shape every area of our lives.

Take heed that thou diligently guardest thy mind.

Listen to Caution

It was late Christmas Eve night, 2004. Well, actually it was early morning. We were all sound asleep—everyone, that is, except Dad. As is his usual Christmas tradition, he was busy finishing up some homemade presents and wrapping all of his last-minute gifts.

The house was quiet, dark, and still—just like Christmas Eve is supposed to be. The clock struck two. Everything was peaceful. The clock struck three. And then something unexpected happened. All of a sudden, as Dad was quietly wrapping his presents, he saw a light turn on in our backyard. Dad stood up, tiptoed to the back door, and peered outside.

The outside light in our backyard is operated by a motion detector. Why would it suddenly turn on? Only motion would do this. But at 3:00 a.m.? Something or *someone* must have set it off. Dad stepped out into the cold air, looked around, and waited silently. He couldn't hear anything. Maybe it was just a stray dog, he figured. But no animals were in sight. After returning to the house to grab a flashlight and put on a coat, he went outside to investigate further. Several minutes later he discovered something curious—footprints in the snow! It appeared as if they had been made by a pair of large boots. Now who would have been going though our backyard at three o' clock on Christmas morning? Something definitely seemed suspicious.

It was possible that the footprints had been made earlier that day or the day before. But Dad was quite sure that the footprints were not from anyone in our family. And, of course, there was still the question of what had set off our motion detector.

Dad went back inside and decided to call the police just to report that he had noticed something suspicious. A friendly policeman stopped by to check things out and assured us that he'd keep a close watch on the neighborhood. He wished Dad a merry Christmas and thanked him for calling. We still don't know why the light mysteriously turned on or who made the footprints. But maybe the motion detector scared whoever or whatever it was away.

A motion detector is designed for both convenience and protection. The one in our backyard provides light to anyone taking the path at night. But, as we learned on Christmas Eve, it is also for protection—sort of like a red flag to inform us that someone is prowling around and we'd better investigate.

In our lives we need to make sure that we have warning systems in place. And when we sense that something is wrong, we need to listen to the caution, stop in our tracks, and check things out. We need to take seriously any small indications that something isn't quite right.

The enemy knows how easily relationships with young men can get out of balance. He knows how quickly we can be distracted. He knows how easy it is for a "just friends" relationship to turn into something romantic. Of course, romance and marriage is God's design for most people, but it needs to occur at the right time, with the right person, and in the right way.

When we're headed in a wrong direction, the Lord will use many different forms of cautions to get our attention. The Holy Spirit will convict us, our consciences will prick us, our parents or friends may point out blind spots or concerns. Much distress will be avoided if we

Anxious maidens must not play with
fire-breathing dragons lest they be burnt.

learn to listen to caution and to act as soon as we realize our error or danger (II Tim. 2:22).

If a friendship is becoming serious when you know it's not the right time, if a friend is encouraging you to compromise your standards, if a relationship is consuming your thoughts or distracting you from your walk with Christ—stop, pray, change course, become accountable to someone, and flee from evil. Don't ignore the red flags that are telling you that something is wrong or that danger is close.

No Vacancies

Spring came and went, but it left behind a lovely yard. My sister Grace went to extra special effort this year to make our yard as beautiful as it could possibly be. My grandma, who is a fabulous gardener, helped a lot as well. Grandma and Grandpa kept dropping over with special deliveries of plants and flowers. And by the time the nicest weather was arriving, everything was just reaching its peak.

God is the One who created beauty. Yet He has given us the job of cultivating and enhancing that which He has created. This takes work. A beautiful garden requires many hours of planning, fertilizing, planting, tending, weeding, and watering. The work is difficult—most people agree that weeding is not very fun. But the final result can be glorious.

In many ways the heart is like a garden. It needs to be protected and kept clean. The good—the beauty, placed there by our heavenly Father—needs to be nurtured. Any pollution needs to be removed. And all enemies—and there are many, coming in all shapes and forms— must be kept away.

Now back to our yard … not only do we have flowers and plants, we also have a variety of wildlife to add excitement to our lives. The rabbits especially seem to be fond of Grace's flowers. We see them everywhere at all hours of the day and night. One little bunny even had the nerve to come right up onto our front porch, stand on its hind legs, stretch over the edge of the flower pot, and nibble the tops of the pink petunias. This may have been rather rude, but it sure was cute! Just as bunnies are seemingly harmless and pleasant but very damaging to plants, so the enemy will attempt to use what is attractive and subtle to destroy the beautiful garden of our heart. Scripture speaks often of how important our heart is in the sight of God. He asks us to keep our hearts clean and pure—free from guilt, wrong motives, and distracting affections (Matt. 5:8, Jas. 4:8). He desires our hearts to be soft—saying that He will not despise a heart that is broken and contrite (Ps. 34:18). He looks for hearts that are tender, upright, sound, and perfect (II Chron. 34:27, Ps. 7:10, Ps. 119:80, II Chron. 16:9). Our heart is the first place the enemy wants to attack. And his tactics may seem harmless, meaningless, and even attractive.

As the flowers were growing and the bunnies were munching in the Mally yard, Mr. and Mrs. Bird were searching for a place to start their family. They also seemed to be excited about Grace's flowers. They began to build their nest in the hanging flower pot over the front step. Imagine Grace's delight a few weeks later when she took the basket down and saw the baby birds. (I hope the birdies were just as delighted with their showers each morning when Mom watered the flowers.) When Grace discovered the nest, she wanted to offer as much help as she could to our little bird family. So she made a small sign and stuck it into the hanging pot. In small, dark letters she wrote the words "No Vacancies."

This also reminds me of our hearts. A heart that is truly guarded must have no vacancies—no empty spaces that need to be filled, no voids that leave open places and room for the enemy to get in. When God asks for our heart, He asks for all of it. He wants to fill every part with Himself. He completes us. Only when we are satisfied in Him will we be able to selflessly give our lives for others. We need to put up a sign that says "No Vacancies." Except we don't need a sign—others will notice simply by our lives. They can see if our heart has voids and is unfulfilled, seeking attention from others, or if we are filled with Jesus, overflowing with love and joy, and seeking to spread His light everywhere we go.

Young ladies who guard their hearts, who are careful in their words and actions, and who know when to be reserved are actually respected by men. I'm not referring to girls who are stand-offish or unapproachable, but rather those who are selfless and sensitive, who display genuine interest in others without thought of attention for themselves. These young ladies gain honor. Young men do not respect girls they can take advantage of—and they do not as easily take advantage of girls they respect. Godly young men are drawn to young ladies who guard their hearts and embrace protection. Immature guys, on the other hand, are often afraid of the girls they respect.

SUGGESTED MEMORY VERSE:

"Keep thy heart with all diligence; for out of it are the issues of life" (Proverbs 4:23).

SUGGESTED ASSIGNMENT:

God does not look at outward appearance; rather, He looks at our hearts. Scripture tells us of a number of different types of "hearts" the Lord is looking for. Get out your Bible and a concordance and make a list of all the various types of "hearts" mentioned in Scripture. Write down any insights you find in these verses (such as rewards God promises or keys to developing a particular type of heart). Then have a time of prayer specifically asking the Lord to give you each one—a pure heart, an upright heart, and so on.

Here are some verses to help you get started:

- I Kings 3:9, 12
- II Chronicles 16:9
- II Chronicles 34:27
- Psalm 7:10
- Psalm 34:18
- Psalm 51:10
- Psalm 119:80
- Proverbs 17:22
- Matthew 5:8
- Matthew 11:29
- Ephesians 4:32
- II Timothy 2:22
- James 4:8
- I Peter 1:22

Making a Commitment of My Own

TESTIMONY BY A YOUNG LADY

On a recent evening I was brushing my teeth and thinking about the events of the day. Specifically, I was thinking about a young lady I knew who had disobeyed her parents and become involved in a relationship with a young man. "How could this have happened so easily?" I wondered. It struck me how easy it is for a girl to fall into a "trap" and forget about her standards just because she likes getting attention from a guy.

As I was brushing my teeth, it dawned on me that although I was planning on courtship and had heard a lot about it, I had never personally made a decision or commitment in this area. I had been struggling in knowing how to respond to a couple guys who liked me, and I suddenly realized that if I gave in and showed attention back, it could lead to more problems and get worse and worse. I knew it would be better for me just to wait and focus on serving the Lord until the time came for me to actually get married. I talked to my mom about it, and she suggested that I make a personal commitment to the Lord. So I kneeled right there against the bathtub ledge and told the Lord that I was making a commitment before Him to not let any kind of relationship develop between me and a young man until my parents and I agree that God is leading me to begin a courtship. Once I had made this decision I felt a sense of freedom that I had never felt in this area before. God's way is always best for us because He loves us so much and wants us to be happy. I am glad I made this commitment while I am still only beginning my teenage years because I know guys can be tempting, and I know it will be the most special if I save my whole heart so that I can give it to my husband on the day I marry.

When I struggle with desiring attention from guys, I think of my commitment to the Lord. *"Let not thine heart envy sinners:*

but be thou in the fear of the Lord all the day long ... Hear thou, my son, and be wise, and guide thine heart in the way" (Prov. 23:17,19).

CHAPTER FOUR

Could He Be the One?

"Be ye not unequally yoked together with unbelievers:
for what fellowship hath righteousness with unrighteousness?
And what communion hath light with darkness?"
II Corinthians 6:14

When the princess returned from the Spring Fair, she told her parents all about her day. They smiled as she described her encounter with the friendly knight and reassured her that she had done the right thing.

Her father told her that every true knight desires a rose that is pure and has kept itself closed. He advised her that she must not be deceived by fancy words but must learn to look at the life, the actions, and the character of any prince who might seek her hand. Her mother reminded her not to worry about it or wonder if she had offended him. "You were not rude, so you must not be concerned about whether he felt welcome, appreciated, or hurt," she said. "Pleasing him is neither your responsibility nor your goal."

The princess tried to forget about the knight, but somehow he seemed to be standing nearby nearly every time she and her mother went to the village, and he was always quick to begin conversing with the princess.

Even so, great was the surprise of both the princess and her parents when Sir Eloquence arrived at the castle saying he wished for her hand in marriage!

The king, desiring to get better acquainted, invited him to spend the day at the castle. Upon closer scrutiny, it became obvious that he was not a real prince, although he might pass for one if seen walking down the road. His armor did not have a proper fit—likely borrowed and not his own. It did not shine in the sun, and he was not accustomed to its weight. Nevertheless, the princess did find herself feeling comfortable in his presence, for he certainly made her feel important and gave the most diligent attention to her every need.

When the king and the queen asked of his adventures, Sir Eloquence was quick to recount his bravery, courage, and heroic victories. But the king told the princess that his stories did not have the sound and character of authentic experience. In fact, he had no evidence that they were even true.

The knight spoke many flattering words to the princess the few times he was able to talk to her with no one else around. He said he could never love any other besides her. The princess was quite confused. But her father was resolute.

Bewildered and a little afraid, the princess stepped outside to take a walk beside the castle walls. She had not gone far when she heard the all too familiar voice of the alligator.

"I hear of the special visitor who came to request thy hand in marriage. Hast thou answered him yet?"

"No, not yet."

"But you will surely say yes. Let me be the first to offer you my congratulations!" declared the alligator with his sharp teeth showing.

"No, I cannot say yes to such a man."

"What?" asked the alligator in surprise. "You will turn down such an opportunity?"

Could He Be the One?

"Opportunity? I consider it more of a trap," stated the princess as she tossed a few stones into the moat and watched the water ripple. She felt like throwing one at the alligator, but decided it wouldn't do much good.

"Why, Princess, thou speakest too rashly. Give him some time at least. Do you not know that all the maidens in the village would give the world for such a prince? Will you decline this handsome prince who loves you, in exchange for the Prince Charming of your dreams who does not even exist? Your standards are too high. You will regret your loss forever."

"My father says he is not a real prince at all."

"Do you not see that your father simply cannot understand?" asked the alligator gently. *"He remembers the old days; he doesn't know how things work in these modern times of change. He does not know the love you have in your heart for the knight."*

"I do not love him!" she declared.

"How would you know? Perhaps you will not let yourself love him. But you must give him a chance. Surely you cannot expect your father to understand. There comes a time when you must decide for yourself. The choice is yours."

"Yes, the choice is mine," said the princess, *"and I have no option but to decline. I would rather never marry at all than marry a man I do not respect."*

"Perhaps thou art afraid," offered the alligator. *"I can understand that you might be timid; after all, you have not had many experiences while hiding here in the castle all of your life. But will you choose now to live in regret the remainder of your life?"*

"No, and because I shall choose not to live in regret, my only option is to decline. In fact, Mr. Alligator, you have made my decision easier. I clearly see now that I would not be happy if I were married to such a man. I think I shall tell my father immediately. Good evening!"

With resolve, the princess hurried to speak to her father. Nearing the west tower, she found him already conversing with the knight.

"I have a challenge for thee," her father was saying. *"How would you like a royal assignment from the king?"*

"I offer my willing service, Your Majesty," Sir Eloquence replied.

"Very good," said the king. "My desire is as follows: I have been hearing reports of one Mr. Scornful who operates a store in the mountain village. It is said that he frequently travels from place to place spreading slander and lies about the upright. His shameless attitude is both contagious and damaging. I would like my citizens to see his true cowardice. Therefore, I propose that you challenge him to a—"

"A debate! What a splendid idea," Eloquence said excitedly, forgetting that interrupting the king is not the most advisable thing to do.

"Nay, sir," said the king with a smile. "Not a fight of mere words, but rather a test of courage and skill."

"You mean—"

"A jousting match. Mr. Scornful boasts frequently of his outstanding *ability, and as of yet, none have been willing to challenge him."*

For a brief moment, Sir Eloquence's face gave the appearance of alarm and distress, but he recovered quickly and began a most articulate discourse.

"Ah, of course, meeting face to face in proper combat is thy intention. A brilliant plan, Sire. And yet, may I suggest that the honor of such a fight belongs to one of the more noble knights—perhaps Sir Valiant, Knight Trueblood, or Prince Gallant. I would not dream of taking the opportunity away from them."

"True, Mr. Scornful is experienced and skillful with the lance and the shield," replied the king, "but he is fearful and cowardly. A fight with him will be easily won. There is no need to defer to those you deem greater."

"Nay," said Sir Eloquence, "for Mr. Scornful is a liar and a cheater at best. He never plays by the rules. Whoever challenges him places himself in a most vulnerable position."

"Most certainly, there is risk involved. Yet if the kingdom is in

danger because of his mocking influence and lies, must he not be stopped? For the sake of the truth, Sir Eloquence. For the sake of the kingdom. Surely personal risk must not be considered."

"Indeed," said Sir Eloquence, "sacrifice and courage must always prevail. In this you are unquestionably correct—and yet we still must be wise in our dealings with such a fellow. Why risk loss, if the risk be not necessary? It is not my own safety that concerns me, but rather the thought of disgrace for the kingdom. A debate would be a certain win. For I am quick with the tongue and eloquent in speech, whereas jousting is not my greatest strength."

"Perhaps," said the king with obvious discernment, "it is because thou hast had more practice with one than the other. What then is your answer? A match or no?"

"I must take time to consider," muttered Sir Eloquence, lacking his usual confidence.

"Farewell then," said the king. "Return when thou canst display in thy life that of which thou boastest in thy words."

Sir Eloquence left the castle without so much as a good-bye to the princess. He seemed to have lost his interest in winning her hand. She was surprised, but grateful that the incident had come to an end so quickly.

Late in the evening, the princess sat down on a stone bench at the edge of the garden. As she watched the fireflies beginning to appear, she thought about the qualities she desired in a husband. Suddenly feeling a strong hand on her shoulder, the princess looked up and saw her father, his tender face illuminated by the bright moonlight. The king sat down beside her, but said nothing.

"I was planning to say no to him anyway," she commented after a few minutes.

"Yes, I know," replied the king, "but I wanted him to realize that smooth speech is not enough to win a princess."

"Nor to win a war," she added. "But father, I certainly intended no harm to come to Sir Eloquence. Would a jousting match have been quite safe?"

"Mr. Scornful would never have actually agreed to a jousting match," the king replied with a chuckle. "For though he often boasts

of his skill, he is a coward at heart. Indeed, even if he were to consent to the match, Sir Eloquence would have been in no danger."

The princess smiled, feeling more assured than ever that she would wait for God's best and settle for no other.

Not Every Knight Wears Shining Armor

I am greatly encouraged by the testimonies of the many young ladies I know who have chosen to stand alone in their commitment to not date. However, I am concerned to see that many of these young ladies seem to have the idea that the first young man who comes along and asks to court them must be *the one*. Just because a young man approaches your father in a "right" way doesn't make him the right one. He may say that he's 100% sure that you are the right one for him, but you must have peace and be sure in your own mind and heart. Do not respond out of fear that there may not be another. And don't be too easy to catch! I'm not saying to be purposely hard, either. This is not a game, and we are definitely not attempting to manipulate. My point is that we need to be wise and honest—if he is not the right one, then we need to say no. If you can't say no, then let your dad do it.

Whenever a young man expresses interest in you, it can be rather flattering. And, naturally, you may feel that you don't want to hurt him. Certainly, we want to handle each situation as carefully and considerately as possible. Yet it is also necessary to realize that Satan will often bring along his "best" before God brings along *His* best. It is essential that you purpose in advance, before there is a young man in the picture, to marry only a Christian—a *strong* Christian. It is also important that you consider what other qualifications you believe are necessary for your future husband.

BE NOT UNEQUALLY YOKED

The Bible clearly teaches that a Christian is to marry only a Christian:

"Be ye not unequally yoked together with unbelievers: for what fellowship hath righteousness with unrighteousness?" (II Cor. 6:14)

"The wife is bound by the law as long as her husband liveth; but if

her husband be dead, she is at liberty to be married to whom she will; only in the Lord" (I Cor. 7:39, emphasis added).

When you get married, your goal becomes to please your husband (I Cor. 7:34). He is your head, your leader, and your authority (Eph. 5:22–24). Think about what would happen if you married someone who was not a believer. How could you submit to a man who did not make his decisions based on the Word of God? What if your husband disliked church and refused to teach your children about Christ? Can you imagine how miserable it would be to use your life to serve someone who didn't have the same goals, the same priorities, or even the same basic foundation that you have?

I know girls who have found themselves in this exact situation. Vicki, for example, started to date a nice young man named Christopher. She wasn't sure if he was a Christian—he certainly wasn't a very strong Christian, but she was hoping to have an opportunity to lead him to the Lord. Soon they were best friends. They did everything together. At first, Vicki didn't realize how attached they had become, but one day she faced reality and determined that she couldn't stand the thought of breaking up now. Vicki decided that since they loved each other so much, everything else would work out. She assumed that after they were married she would be able to encourage him to get involved in church and grow in the Lord.

They got married, yet their marriage wasn't a happy one. He was interested in her—but not in Christ. Now he felt "pushed" to Christ and didn't like it. Instead of listening to Vicki when she tried to encourage him in spiritual things, he went in the opposite direction—away from the Lord. And of course, he did not provide the kind of spiritual leadership in the home that a father must provide. In the end, despite Vicki's effort to lead her children to Christ, some of her kids followed their father, and she felt like she had used her life to raise a generation of non-Christians. This story is a tragedy. And it's happening all around us.

MARRY A STRONG CHRISTIAN

It was the Fourth of July, and my sister Grace and I were mingling among the crowds who had gathered downtown. We have found that early evening on Independence Day is an ideal time to hand out tracts, get into witnessing conversations, and share the gospel. Crowds of people are just sitting around with nothing much to do as they wait for the fireworks to start. Many of them are happy to talk. As I wandered along asking the Lord to direct me to the right people, I noticed a couple of families sitting on lawn chairs, chatting, eating snacks, and looking rather bored. As I walked by, I told them I was taking my own personal "survey" and wondered if I could ask them a few questions. They smiled a little suspiciously, but seemed very willing to talk. However, as soon as they found out that I was a Christian, they began to fire away with all the common arguments non-Christians use to attack the Bible. Before I knew it, we were having a friendly, yet intense, debate. Then one lady threw an argument at me that I wasn't expecting: "The Bible teaches that Christians can marry only Christians, right?"

"Yes."

"Well, think of how limited you are. My daughter can pick any guy she wants for a husband, but you have only a small selection!"

I can't remember how I answered her at the time, but I laughed afterwards. She doesn't know how truly limited I am. More than she could guess! Hopefully, you, just like me, want a lot more in a husband than simply a professing Christian. That lady should see our list of qualifications! What she doesn't understand is that we wouldn't *want* anything less. It's not that we're *limited* to a few—rather, we're *thrilled* to know that a strong Christian is the best of the best! We have so much to look forward to as Christians preparing for a happy, fulfilling marriage built upon Christ. The best the unsaved world offers doesn't even compare.

Since each of us wants to have the best marriage possible, we need to marry not just any Christian, but a strong Christian. Do you want to use your life to serve the Lord? Is your primary goal to seek first the kingdom of God and His righteousness? Your husband needs to have the same vision, commitments, and life purpose that you have. And vice versa.

EVALUATE HIS CHARACTER AND DIRECTION

"Well, what should I say to this?" I asked Mom and Dad one day as I was reading my e-mails. "I just got an e-mail from 'so and so,' asking if he can get to know me better." He was a godly young man who was a few years older than I was, but he wasn't someone in whom I thought I would be interested. "How do you think I should answer him?" I asked. My parents didn't know this young man very well and asked me what I thought of him. I answered that he seemed to be a nice guy, but I did not believe he was the right one for me.

As Mom, Dad, and I discussed this possibility, my dad suggested, "Why don't you make a list of the qualifications you are looking for in a husband?" He went on to say, "I'd encourage you to make two lists: a list of the **essential** qualities—things that you consider a requirement for marriage, and a list of the **desirable** qualities—things that are important to you, though not necessarily a requirement." Then my parents decided that they would make two such lists as well. We worked individually, came together with our lists in hand, and then compared notes.

This was a helpful exercise, and by the time we were finished, we all agreed that this particular young man was not the right one for me. Since we already had peace about this decision, we agreed that there was no need for me to get to know him better. Rather, it would simply be a distraction for me and probably for him as well.

I would encourage you to make two similar lists. Be specific. If you have thought through your qualifications in advance and written a list, it will be a safeguard to keep you from being captivated or ensnared by someone who comes along but who may not have the spiritual strength to which you are committed. Then ask your parents to make a list. Compare them. You might find that some things your parents consider important are areas that have never even crossed your mind.

SURELY THIS MUST BE THE ONE

What are you looking for in a husband? Do you remember the story of when God told Samuel to anoint one of the sons of Jesse to be King of Israel? When Samuel saw Eliab, the firstborn, he was impressed. Seeing that he was tall, mature, and handsome, he thought, *"Surely, this must be the one." But the Lord told Samuel, "Look not on his countenance, or on the height of his stature: because I have refused him: for the Lord seeth not as man seeth; for man looketh on the outward appearance, but the Lord looketh on the heart"* (I Sam. 16:6–7).

It is easy for us to be like Samuel. We look at outward things. We notice someone who is handsome and popular, who sounds impressive, and who seems to be respected by everyone else. We look for Eliabs. But pray, rather, for a man after God's own heart—pray for a David. Pray for a man whose life is devoted to the Lord so that as you give yourself to him, you will be using your life to bring forth fruit that is eternal. Pray for a man who loves Christ more than he loves you. Pray for a man upon whom God's blessing is evident.

Here are just a few qualifications to consider for your list:

- Does he have assurance of eternal life?
- Does he faithfully share the gospel with others?
- Is he always truthful?
- Is he committed to never being divorced?
- Does he honor his parents?
- Has he applied diligence in spiritual disciplines such as Bible reading, prayer, fasting, memorization, and giving?
- Does he make all decisions based upon the Word of God?
- Would you be excited to have him as the father of your children?
- Is he diligent in his work and wise in his use of money?
- Is God calling you in the same direction of ministry?
- Does he ask forgiveness when he is wrong?
- Is he humble and willing to be a servant?
- Is he kind, thoughtful, and gracious?
- Is he generous with others?
- Does he respond to criticism in a Christlike way?
- Is he willing to stand alone?
- Do you see spiritual fruit in his life?

Rescue thou not the first maiden in distress.

Most importantly, I encourage you to look for fruit in a young man's life. Anybody can talk. Look at his actions. It's not enough that he simply *says* he wants to serve the Lord; you need to see spiritual *fruit* in his life. If there is already fruit, then you know he's serious about his walk with the Lord (Matt. 7:16–20). Now, I suppose some girls might say, "Oh, my boyfriend has ministry. He has a cross on his T-shirt!" or, "He has a bumper sticker on his car that says, 'Honk if you love Jesus.' " That is not exactly what I have in mind. Look for evidence of lasting fruit—both in his life and in his ministry. Does he exhibit the fruit of the Spirit (Gal. 5:22–23)? Do you know people he has led to the Lord or people he has discipled? Have you seen God at work both in him and through him?

This may require some waiting on your part! After all, a young man will probably change a lot between the ages of eighteen and twenty-three. We know young men who seemed to be doing well when they were eighteen, but are not living for the Lord today. It is often better to wait a few years until a young man is further into his life work and you can see visible success and fruit in his life. I'm not saying that it is wrong to get married young. My emphasis is not on *age*, but on *spiritual maturity* and *fruit*.

Is this standard too high? Is it unrealistic to commit to marrying only a strong Christian who is devoted to the Lord? Does this type of man even exist any more? Must we actually wait until we see fruit in a young man's life?

Well, think of it this way. For the *world*, this standard is not too high. In fact, many fathers have said to their daughters, "You're not marrying that guy until he finishes school and is successful and has a respectable job and a good paycheck coming in—then you can marry him." You see, when it comes to money, the standard is not too high. In the same way, shouldn't we, who are committed to the Lord and His ways, be willing to make spiritual things our priority?

Knock-knock. We answered the door and found an excited friend bringing some interesting news. "Sarah, I found the perfect young

Know also that not by every knight is it worth being rescued.

man for you. He works at a car shop where I recently got my van fixed. He doesn't drink, he doesn't smoke, and he's very polite. I think he'd even be willing to go to church with you."

She was so enthused that I didn't want to just come out and tell her that I … uh … well, I have a lot more requirements besides not drinking and not smoking. So I simply said, "Well, I'm not really looking for a husband. I'm … just … trusting that God will bring it about in His timing."

"But maybe God is using me!" she continued excitedly. "Perhaps you're frightened, Sarah," she offered. "I'd be happy to arrange a way for you to meet him. How about if you come with me? I'll take you to meet him right now. I've already told him about you."

My family listened with amusement as I reiterated a little more strongly how I really wanted to let the Lord give direction in this area of marriage. I also began to explain that I desired a husband who was committed to using his life for the Lord's work. It took a lot more explaining before I finally convinced her that I wasn't interested. But as she left, she urged me to try to meet him as soon as possible.

Don't expect others to understand the commitments to which the Lord has led you. God's ways often seem foolish to the world. Surprisingly, the church itself is frequently slow to receive many Biblical convictions. Actually, many times we may get the most resistance from well-meaning Christian friends or relatives. The world misunderstood Jesus too. They laughed at the prophets. They rejected the apostles. We're in good company. Strive to love and accept others who misunderstand you, but never be afraid to face criticism for standing alone.

Are You Ready for Marriage?

If you are not ready for marriage, then there is no good reason to begin to develop a relationship leading in that direction. Of course, I doubt that any of us are actually ever *fully ready* to get married, but here are some questions to ask yourself:

- Do I have assurance of eternal life? Do I know the Lord as my personal Savior?

- Do I have a clear conscience? Is there anything in my life that needs to be cleared up, confessed, or corrected?
- Am I "about my Father's business"? Have I been diligent to complete the tasks the Lord has given me?
- Do I have a good relationship with my parents and siblings?
- Have I learned to be a servant by seeing and meeting the needs of others before my own?
- Have I learned to overcome anger?
- Are there people who have offended me whom I am not able to forgive?
- Do I read my Bible daily?
- Do I find myself often in prayer, consulting with God and enjoying close, intimate conversations with Him?
- Have I been diligent to identify and develop the skills, ministry, and interests God has given me?
- Have I learned basic life skills, both educational ones and practical responsibilities?
- Am I able to take care of a household?
- Am I ready to be a mother?
- Have I learned to be a giver, not a taker, in relationships?

My friend Karen longed to be married. As she neared her late twenties, she began to wonder if God would ever answer her prayers and provide a godly husband. She tried to be patient, but it was hard not to worry. Then one day Karen met a nice man at a church singles group who seemed to be a perfect match for her. He expressed interest, and the two of them began to date. But as Karen got to know him better, she began to have second thoughts about their relationship. He was a Christian, but he had been divorced and didn't really have the spiritual strength she was looking for in a mate.

Now, as she looks back on this situation, she recognizes that the enemy offered his best before God brought along *His* best. But of course, she couldn't see that at the time, and the temptation seemed nearly impossible to resist. As their relationship grew more and more serious, the Lord began to bring stronger cautions into her life. Her pastor and others from her church warned her of this man's weaknesses and encouraged her to break up with him.

Karen struggled. Would she ever get married? She was already close to thirty. This might be her only chance! After much prayer and many tears, she purposed to obey the Lord and to break up—even if it meant that she would never get married at all. She began to pray Psalm 37:3–5, asking the Lord for the strength to be faithful, to trust, and to delight herself in Him.

Shortly after her decision to break off the relationship that she knew was not God's best, the Lord brought George into her life. He was so much better than the man she had been dating before, she could hardly believe this was happening to her! He was on fire for the Lord and preparing to be a pastor. Today they have three children and continue to serve the Lord together faithfully.

If we truly want God's best, it usually requires patience on our part. Believe me—Karen is glad that she waited!

Know thou assuredly that not every
knight weareth shining armor.

SUGGESTED MEMORY VERSE:

"Be ye not unequally yoked together with unbelievers: for what fellowship hath righteousness with unrighteousness? And what communion hath light with darkness?" (II Corinthians 6:14).

SUGGESTED ASSIGNMENT:

As explained on pages 76–77, make a list of the qualities that you consider essential for your future husband and then a list of the non-essential but desirable ones. Ask your parents to make these two lists as well. Compare and discuss them. As you consider qualities for your list, examine how Scripture describes some of the great men of God.

For example:
- Job was a man who was blameless and upright, who feared the Lord and turned away from evil (Job 1:1).
- Caleb is described numerous times as one who wholly followed the Lord (Josh. 14:14).
- David was a man after God's own heart. He was skillful, a mighty man of valor, prudent in speech, and the Lord was with him (I Sam. 16:18).
- Daniel purposed that he would not defile himself (Dan. 1:8).
- Stephen was a man full of faith, power, wisdom, and the Holy Spirit (Acts 6).

CHAPTER FIVE

Romantic Dreams

"Finally, brethren, whatsoever things are true,
whatsoever things are honest, whatsoever things are just,
whatsoever things are pure, whatsoever things are lovely,
whatsoever things are of good report; if there be any virtue,
and if there be any praise, think on these things."
Philippians 4:8

"Art thou coming with me, dear?" the queen asked.

"Yes, Mother, but I hope I do not see Sir Eloquence in town today. I wish everybody would stop asking me about him."

The princess was glad that the knight had stopped pursuing her hand, and she did not expect him to be bothering her in the village anymore. Yet, now that he was gone, she did miss him just a little bit—or maybe it was simply his affectionate words and attention that she sometimes wished for ....

"Stop worrying about him, dear. Thy father and I are proud of thy

decision. You never have to fear what others think when you know you have done what is right."

"I know, Mother. But no one understands why I do not go to any of the dances or parties. They say I will never meet anyone and that I do nothing but sit in the castle and dream."

"Nay, my daughter, they admire thy beauty, thy graciousness, and, most of all, thy purity. A few will always criticize. Perhaps they are jealous. In addition, it is likely that they feel guilty due to their own carelessness, and rather than changing their ways, they think it easier to find fault with any who take the narrow way."

"But they speak lies of me," said the princess. "Instead of being a candle as Father says, I fear that I am merely discouraging any from following the way of purity. Everyone says my example is foolish and ridiculous."

"Not so, for many more respect thy ways than thou knowest. But as a crow cries noisily and interrupts an otherwise peaceful world, so the few critics are usually verbal while the many admirers remain silent."

"But I must explain my motives. I must tell them that the rumors they hear are false."

"Oh no, thou canst not defend thyself," explained her mother. "It will only give credence to the lies. A princess must let her life and good works be her defense against any who seek to slander."

"Well, I suppose—" began the princess, but suddenly she exclaimed, "Oh, look Mother, there is my friend, Maiden Flirtelia. I have not seen her in weeks."

"Yes, it would be nice for you to visit with her," spoke her mother. "I shall meet you at Fountain Circle after lunch."

* * *

"Well, good afternoon, Princess," said her friend. "You look lovely today."

"Oh, thank you, Flirtelia. How good to see you!"

Maiden Flirtelia and the princess spent the next few hours looking around Market Street, visiting the tapestry shop, and picking up some pastries at the bakery. Then they sat down at Fountain Circle to talk.

"I must tell you, I had the most wonderful time last evening at the Summer Ball," Flirtelia chattered excitedly. *"You should have been there to meet all the enchanting young men. I had such a romantic time with Sir Striking."*

"Oh, Flirtelia, thou hast not changed at all! Can you think of nothing else besides men, romance, parties, and weddings?"

"And you have not changed at all either," Maiden Flirtelia replied. *"Will you ever grow up and start enjoying your life? In fact, I heard that Sir Eloquence was seeking thy hand. I cannot believe you would not even take time to consider him. Dost thou not know that he is one of the most popular knights?"*

"Why take time for something one already knows will come to nothing, especially when it is neither wise nor safe?" asked the princess.

"Well then, you could have at least suggested that he get to know **me***!"* declared Flirtelia.

"You may suggest it to him yourself if you like," said the princess with a smile. *"You seem to have ample opportunities to converse with the knights."*

"Art thou saying that thou hast no opportunities? You really should come to one of the dances. I'll arrange a match for you."

"No really, Flirtelia, you just do not understand, do you?"

"Understand?" asked Maiden Flirtelia. *"No, I do not understand! Why would you say no to such a choice knight? Why would you miss out on so many fun and harmless activities? No, I do not understand at all!"*

As they spoke, they were interrupted by a company of horsemen who came galloping into town. They rode quickly, on urgent business for the king, but they stopped briefly to make a proclamation. The princess and Flirtelia stood up and joined the crowd that had gathered to hear the message. It was then that the princess caught her first glimpse of Sir Valiant. He was well known in the kingdom for his heroic deeds, and well respected for his loyalty to the king. The princess had heard her father speak of him before, but never had she known that he was so handsome or youthful. With dignity he spoke to the people, and with a sparkle in his eyes he bade them farewell. The princess could not help

but notice that he far surpassed the other knights she knew in word and conduct ... yes ... he was so very ...

"Oh there you are, dear," said her mother, interrupting her thoughts. "Dear?" she said again, trying to get her attention.

"Oh, sorry," replied the princess. "You were talking to me? I was, um, thinking of something else."

"I am returning home now. Art thou ready?"

"Why yes, I guess."

All the way home the princess was thinking. With fresh and new expectancy, all her dreams were coming back: romance, falling in love, living happily ever after with ... with ... with someone like Sir Valiant.

Toward evening she decided to go out for a stroll. As usual, she was not alone. "Well, well, it is you again," announced the alligator. "Staring up at the stars? I suppose you are still sure you made the right decision about Sir Eloquence?"

"Yes, very."

"I marvel at thy innocence. And I fear for it. Thou art no longer a mere sixteen, young and sweet. Thou art nearing eighteen. It is time to become thine own boss."

The princess said nothing, her blue eyes gazing at the glistening moon.

"I wonder what thou art thinking about," probed the alligator.

"The stars are beautiful," the princess replied softly.

"You are quiet tonight," he said, trying to sound tender.

"Perhaps thou shouldest be too," she answered in a tone that did not reveal whether she was amused or annoyed.

"Thou art deep in thought," continued the alligator. "About something ... or maybe someone? Listen to me, Princess, it is not too late to tell Sir Eloquence that you have changed your mind. You think your father will not let you. But Princess, you are free to do as you wish. You could leave the castle this very night."

"Really, I marvel at thy ignorance," she replied. "Art thou too blind to see that I never have, nor ever will, love a man like him?"

"Then what kind of man wilt thou love?"

"Someone heroic and valiant, not merely skilled in speech.

Someone who is kind and pure in heart. Someone who does not play with white roses that belong to others."

"Dreams are good. But you must learn to give up certain ideals in order to face reality," he said insistently.

"And treat casually what ought to be treasured and protected?"

"Princess, thou art too careful. Thou art afraid to try anything new. One little mistake will not matter."

"There is no such thing as a little sin," she declared. "Good night!"

Daydreaming of Knights

Most young princesses have spent at least a few evenings of their lives looking at the stars, thinking, dreaming, wondering, imagining, and asking the Lord about their futures. There is nothing unusual about having questions about what might be in store for us—and *who* might be in store for us—but we often find that the enemy will use this area to distract us from our focus on Christ.

Not only do our own thoughts easily drift toward romance, but there seem to be plenty of other people out there anxious to "help" us be distracted by guys. After all, starting in preschool, well-meaning adults and relatives begin asking us if we have a boyfriend. Then, to make matters worse, the majority of girls we meet seem to be anxious to tell us about their special someone, or quick to point out whichever guy they presently think is the cutest.

In addition to our own struggle with thoughts and the influence of friends is the fact that sooner or later we are going to meet a guy that we … or at least that we *think* we … or, well, a guy that we *wonder* if … Okay, a guy that we *like*—or should I say LIKE! Now what?

WHAT IF I HAVE A CRUSH?

Have you ever made your dad panic?

Once when I was about eight years old, I scampered into the house and with a mischievous smile I announced, "Dad, I fell in love today!"

Believe me, that got his attention! He looked up at me with a worried expression on his face and said, "You did?"

"Yep! I fell in love with this adorable Dalmatian puppy at the pet store. Can I get it? Please?" Dad smiled with a look of relief.

I never got the Dalmatian puppy, but as could be expected, I eventually got older and found myself noticing more than just cute Dalmatian puppies. How should a girl respond to a crush? Well, first of all, let me reassure you that nearly every girl gets one from time to time. It's easy to notice guys, and if we see a young man that we like, it's natural to find ourselves thinking about him.

Don't panic just because you find yourself noticing a guy. It's normal. You don't need to try to convince yourself that you don't actually have a crush or to deceive yourself that you don't really like him. The problem isn't so much *having* a crush, but how we respond to it.

One of the annoying things about crushes is that they happen quickly. We meet a young man, and before we even get to know him, we find ourselves daydreaming about him, attaching our first name to his last name to see how it sounds, and choosing the colors of our bridesmaids' dresses. As soon as we realize what we're doing, we're horrified, since after all, we hardly even *know* him. Feeling embarrassed by our own foolishness, we purpose not to let our minds wander that way ever again. But five minutes later we suddenly realize that we've just been dreaming about "so and so" all over again, wondering what our kids would look like, or choosing which flowers we'd like at our wedding. In frustration, we wonder how to stop this pattern.

When I was about thirteen, our family became acquainted with another Christian family who had a son a few years older than I was. I liked him right away. He seemed so considerate and nice. I admired some of his talents, and most of all, he seemed like such a strong Christian leader. He was the first guy that I ever really liked, and I felt so embarrassed. I didn't want anyone to know how I felt about him. After all, I was only thirteen! I wasn't considering getting married for years. I tried to avoid him so that no one would guess that I was attracted to him. I tried not to talk about him with my family or others because I was worried that they might be able to figure out that I liked him.

But inwardly I was struggling. Even though I didn't see him very often, I frequently found myself wondering when I might see him again and questioning if he could be the right one for me. I remember that when I would practice the piano, ride my bike, or have spare time, I would frequently be struggling with these thoughts and asking the Lord to help me not be so distracted.

A few years later I got to know this young man a little bit better and realized that he was definitely not the right one for me. I lost interest, but I wondered when my next crush might happen and if I would be able to handle it any better.

So What Should I Do?

First of all, I have some suggestions of what **not** to do when you have a crush:
- Don't talk about him with your friends.
- Don't intentionally do anything that will stir up more thoughts about him (i.e. don't put pictures of him up on your wall ☺).
- Don't tell him how you feel about him or give any indications that you might be interested.
- Don't dwell on thoughts of him or let yourself get carried away with your dreamy imaginations.

Rather, when thoughts about young men arise (and they will), use these as a springboard to direct you to pray and delight in the Lord. Several young ladies have told me that they choose specific targets, such as an unsaved friend or a leader in authority, and purpose to pray for this individual every time they are distracted by wrong thoughts. The enemy is going to think twice about stirring up vain thoughts when he realizes that every time the thought comes, you simply turn it into a prayer. Another idea is to simply pray for the particular young man—that he would be strong in the Lord and faithful in bringing forth much fruit. When struggling with thoughts, I sometimes have begun to pray for my future husband even though I don't know who he will be. Also, I use distracting thoughts about young men to remind me to delight in the Lord and to look forward to the coming of my true Prince. *"Looking for that blessed hope, and the glorious appearing of the great God and our Savior Jesus Christ"* (Tit. 2:13).

A second way to deal with crushes is to talk to your parents about it. This might be difficult, scary, or embarrassing for you, but most likely your parents have already guessed how you are feeling. If you tell them, they will be better able to pray for, protect, and advise you. Confiding in your parents often relieves the pressure on you and may lighten the intensity of your "secret" crush. Sometimes they are able to help you think more realistically about your future and give you a new perspective about what type of man they believe the Lord has in store for you.

Several times when I have told my dad or brother that I have noticed a certain young man, they have said that if they get a convenient opportunity they will try to get to know him better. Often they are able to come up with interesting observations that I didn't see, and they come to me saying, "Sarah, have you noticed this area?" Dad will usually say, "I question 'such and such.'" My brother Stephen will say, "He's kinda weird!" But I'm serious—dads and brothers can be great analytical agents! When they notice an area of weakness in a

Rely thou not solely on feelings or emotions

young man, it gives me a clearer perspective of the whole situation and makes it easier for me to stay focused on the Lord, rather than dreaming about the possibility of "so and so." It frees me from any pressure or temptation I might be feeling to try to get to know him better, and keeps my emotions from getting involved unnecessarily.

And finally, when you are struggling with a crush, exercise faith by purposing to wait for the Lord. If this young man you are thinking about is the right one for you, God has apparently already started the work of bringing you together and will fulfill what He has begun in His perfect time and way. You don't need to do anything. In fact, it will be most perfect if you just stay out of the way while the Lord works! And if he is not the right one for you, then you certainly don't want to initiate anything to bring about a relationship. So either way, whether he *is* or *is not* God's choice for you, your responsibility is to trust God in the area of marriage, treat the young man in the same way as you would treat any other brother in Christ, and focus on the Lord and doing His will.

After all, your life is not really your story—it's God's story. You belong to Him. You represent Him. He is the One who gets the credit and the glory for your life. Do not pray for your own desires to come to pass. Pray for ultimate glory to be given to Jesus. That's what you really want—isn't it? And remember, ultimate glory for Jesus means ultimate joy for you.

Surrounded by Alligators

In the world in which we live, I'm sure you agree that it's difficult to keep our thoughts pure. With everyone talking about romance all the time, worldly pictures posted everywhere you look, inappropriate music playing in stores, and the constant bombardment of temptations from magazines, the Internet, billboards, and television, it certainly doesn't seem easy to apply Philippians 4:8 and think about that which is true, honest, just, pure, lovely, and of good report.

THOUGHTS ABOUT THOUGHTS

"Can I talk to you for a minute, Sarah?" a young lady asked me recently.

"Well," she began, "I have this uh … problem … and I'm really struggling. I … you see, I've made a decision not to date, and I want to wait for God to bring the right husband … but I, uh … I don't know if anyone else has this problem, but, well, I've really been struggling with … with my thoughts. I mean, I might be keeping myself physically pure, but how do I keep myself emotionally pure? What if I give my heart away just by thinking about someone too much? And how do I know if I'm guarding my heart? Is it possible to control my thoughts? This has been a big problem for me for a long time."

I smiled a little. "Well, first off, Kate, let me tell you that you are not the only girl who has this problem," I said. "I've been asked that question before. Lots of times. Many young ladies have told me that controlling their thoughts is their biggest struggle. In fact, at one Bright Lights meeting (to learn about the Bright Lights ministry, see pages 253–256) where we had been discussing cleanliness, I asked each girl to write on a slip of paper what area of her life was hardest to keep 'clean.' As I collected the slips and read their answers, I found that 'keeping thoughts pure' was the most common struggle. The more I have talked with young ladies, the more I have found this to be the case."

"Really?" Kate said. "Well, it's good to hear that I'm not the *only* girl with this problem."

The way Kate worded it made me smile again. "No, you're definitely not the only one. But Satan wants you to think you are. He wants us to feel defeated and to think that we have failed. But the Bible says, *'There hath no temptation taken you but such as is common to man: but God is faithful, who will not suffer you to be tempted above that ye are able; but will with the temptation also make a way to escape, that ye may be able to bear it'"* (I Cor. 10:13).

Kate and I went on to discuss thoughts and how we should deal with them. Satan works hard to deceive, confuse, and pollute us with wrong thoughts. It is not merely crushes that we face. Satan attacks in many different ways with thoughts that are vain, wicked, covetous, bitter, and untrue. Imagine for a moment that your mind is a battlefield. If you are a Christian, the battlefield belongs to Jesus—it is His territory. We are commanded to take captive every thought to the obedience of Christ (II Cor. 10:5). We may not be able to determine what thoughts come into our minds, but we **can** determine what we do with those thoughts.

Sometimes "enemy thoughts" are obvious, but other times they are disguised in ways we won't easily recognize. If we allow them to stay, they will lead to wrong beliefs, wrong attitudes, wrong actions, and eventually wrong habits. The alligator spoke many lies to the princess. Some of these same lies are ones that we may find ourselves believing. They are subtle, but deadly. It is not enough to just expose or get rid of a wrong thought. We need to replace the lie with truth. God's Word is our standard. We must judge every thought according to the truth of Scripture. Memorize specific verses relating to lies you are tempted to believe. Meditate on these verses whenever you are tempted to believe that particular lie.

FLEE FROM HUMAN WISDOM

Cookies 'n Cream is my favorite flavor of ice cream. Or maybe it's Peanut Butter Cup. I'm not sure. Mint Chip ranks right at the top, too. Well, anyway, I can't remember what kind of ice cream I was eating, but I know that it was in a cone and, as always, it was delicious. The only problem with my cone was that it was dripping. Even worse, it was dripping from more than one place—both the top and the bottom. I was trying to catch the drips as they fell, keep myself clean, and still get a lick from the top every so often, but needless to say, it wasn't working too well. I was getting frustrated, almost upset, at my ice cream cone. After all, cones are not supposed to have holes in the bottom. Finally, I, being a smart seven-year-old, had a brilliant plan. Taking one big mouthful, I bit off the bottom of my cone. I don't know what I was thinking (my younger brother would be quick to point out that I *wasn't thinking*), but it didn't take long for me to realize that this was not such a bright idea. The next thing I remember is that I was holding my cone sideways and trying to eat out of both sides at once. The story only gets worse, so we'll stop here. The point is that we humans often try to come up with our own solutions to life's problems. Our own reasoning simply makes things worse, and the mess we're in only gets messier.

The world doesn't want you to think about the consequences of your actions. Just think about what feels good right now. Don't think about tomorrow. Take a bite. Don't worry about what comes next. The alligator usually did not speak a blatant lie to the princess; rather, he tried to mix a small lie with some truth. In the same way, the world will bombard us with advice and answers that sound pretty safe, logical, and attractive. The enemy encourages us to take the easy way, to follow the crowd, to reject our parents' counsel, to take matters into our own hands, to seek attention for ourselves, and to compromise our standards. The enemy also throws fiery darts of fear and doubt. He tells us that God's ways won't work, that God has forgotten us, that we are a failure, and that God is against us.

These untruths are even more deadly than the fantasizing and dreamy thoughts that result from a crush. When we begin to believe them (usually subconsciously), they *will* affect our actions and attitudes. Wrong thoughts must be brought under the control of God's Word. We must not attempt to use human reasoning to live the Christian life. Proverbs 3:5 says, *"Lean not unto thine own understanding."* Scripture also exhorts us to love the Lord with all our heart, with all our soul, with all our strength, and with all our **mind** (Lk. 10:27, emphasis added). To do this, we must yield not only our lives, but also our minds to the Lord Jesus Christ. Make a conscious decision to place your mind under the authority of God's Word.

If you struggle with thoughts (and we all do), then I cannot emphasize enough how essential it is that you fill your mind with Scripture. Read and memorize it every day. Set a goal to memorize entire books of the Bible. Get into the habit of quoting Scripture during spare moments. Think about it as you are going to sleep at night. Engraft the Word of God into your life so that it becomes a part of you. This paragraph may be the most important one in this book. It is not possible to remove wrong or vain thoughts without replacing them with something else. The only way to get rid of darkness is to fill the space with light!

SUGGESTED MEMORY VERSE:

"Finally, brethren, whatsoever things are true, whatsoever things are honest, whatsoever things are just, whatsoever things are pure, whatsoever things are lovely, whatsoever things are of good report; if there be any virtue, and if there be any praise, think on these things" (Philippians 4:8).

SUGGESTED ASSIGNMENT:

What are some of the specific lies, thoughts, and fears that Satan uses against you? Write down several of them, and then find Scripture verses to combat each wrong thought of the enemy. Memorize these verses and quote them every time you find yourself entertaining fears or believing lies. Here are a few examples of lies we commonly believe contrasted with Biblical truth:

"God has forgotten about me."
"I will never leave thee, nor forsake thee" (Heb. 13:5).

"It's too hard to wait."
"I can do all things through Christ ... " (Phil. 4:13).

"I need to make my own decisions."
"Lean not unto thine own understanding" (Prov. 3:5).

"One little sin won't matter."
"Whatsoever a man soweth, that shall he also reap" (Gal. 6:7).

Before You Meet Prince Charming

When it Seems Too Hard

Testimony by a young lady

It was a huge crush. He was so handsome and so nice. I was in my senior year of high school and had recently become acquainted with a good-looking, intelligent young man who was an incredible pianist. Our piano teacher had us play a duet together, and I soon found myself very attracted to him.

He was not a believer, but he seemed like such a nice guy. We saw each other at various piano competitions and events throughout my senior year and became casual friends.

I really liked him a lot—so much so, that I started daydreaming about him all of the time. He became an idol in my heart, and I felt like I was constantly struggling with my thoughts and desires.

Soon I had become extremely discontent. I determined that if this young man asked me to date him, I would readily accept, even though I would be disobeying God and my parents, damaging my testimony, and endangering my purity. I began to be bitter toward the Lord because the Christian life seemed too hard. I doubted that the Lord was actually being good to me.

Thankfully, God protected me and this young man never asked me to date him. I finally repented of my sin to the Lord and gradually this crush died away.

The Lord has been showing me that even more importantly than guarding my mind from crushes, I need to guard my mind from lies. Satan wants me to think that God doesn't really know what is best for me. It requires faith to believe that the Lord is completely good and absolutely trustworthy. The Lord often reminds me of Psalm 84:11, reassuring me that He only has the very best in store for His servants. *"For the Lord God is a sun and shield: the Lord will give grace and glory: no good thing will He withhold from them that walk uprightly."*

Even though I sometimes think that a boyfriend would be

a "good thing," God knows that having a boyfriend right now would not be a "good thing" for me. I still struggle with being discontent and wanting a boyfriend, especially when friends around me are pairing up, but I have learned that the Lord is everything I need. When I allow myself to become discontent, I simply get more and more depressed, and am useless to the Lord. But when I trust in His faithfulness and power, I find peace and joy. I'm excited to see how the Lord is daily teaching me what it means to guard my heart and mind, and to delight fully in Him.

CHAPTER SIX

When God Says Wait

*"For the Lord God is a sun and shield: the Lord will give
grace and glory: no good thing will He withhold from them
that walk uprightly. O Lord of hosts, blessed is the man
that trusteth in Thee."*
Psalm 84:11–12

The princess thought often of what her father had said about being a
rose and a candle. The alligator was constantly telling her that she
needed to spend more time with the young men in the village and
with the peasants in the country. But she remembered the words of
her father. Just a few weeks previously he had explained to her that
the way to find a mate is not to look—but to prepare. Not to allow
thoughts of worry or fear, but to exercise patience and faith. She knew
he was right. Each day was a gift. She would devote her time to doing
as much as she possibly could for God's glory and continue to wait for

her prince. She began to find increasingly greater joy in serving her father and laying down her life for others.

*Much was being accomplished during this time of her life. The princess often represented the royal family on important occasions, and she spent many days caring for orphaned children in the nearby villages—even beginning a courtyard club for them. Sometimes she would host tea parties, teaching godliness to village girls. God was also teaching **her** much during these years and filling her with understanding and ability in all manner of workmanship. She was gaining skill in many kinds of fabric work, weaving and tapestry, candle work and soap making, as well as fine artistry with dyes, paints, and gold. She did not neglect her writing, archery, or equestrianship, and she also made it a goal to learn the useful talents of floral decorating and baking.*

Many widows and weary mothers were the joyous recipients of homemade gifts or meals from the princess. She tried to use each thing she learned in some way as a tool to accomplish her assignments from her heavenly Father. Each mastery acquired could also then be taught to all the wise-hearted young ladies in the kingdom. Her days were full and fruitful. Many stories, memories, and friendships were hers. In hundreds of little ways, she was a candle spreading light everywhere she went, bringing strength and encouragement to many lives that were filled with darkness.

Days passed. Weeks passed. Months passed. Yes, it was hard to wait, but she was busy with the work she loved. A year passed. She was now nineteen years old. During this time, the princess began to find pleasure in looking out her bedroom window and imagining the day her prince would come. "What will he be like?" she wondered. "When will I meet him? Or have I met him already? I wonder what his first words to me will be? And, oh, what will it be like to fall in love?"

Yet another year passed. The more time she spent looking out the window, the less time she spent listening to her father and focusing on the needs of others. It was during this time that a little seed began to grow in the princess's heart. The seed was called Discontent. At first it was so subtle that she hardly knew it was there. Oh, she would be quick to tell herself that she was happy, trusting her heavenly Father, and willing to wait however long He thought best.

But meanwhile she would often feel hurt when she heard of knights who came for other maidens, and she would find anxiety and even sorrow in her heart as she thought of her own predicament and the dreams that might never be fulfilled. The seed of Discontent grew. The more she looked out the window, the more she felt sorry for herself. And the more she felt sorry for herself, the more she looked out the window.

"What be wrong, dear Princess?" asked the alligator one afternoon. "I can see thou art not as happy as thou always wast."

"What dost thou mean? I be fine!" she replied promptly, flinging her hair behind her shoulder.

"You merely pretend to be happy. Thou art lonely."

She said nothing for a moment, but then acknowledged, "Well, perhaps, sometimes."

"Nay, but all the time. And you will always be lonely, for you will always be alone. Thinkest that a prince will be coming for you? Foolish Princess, thou must be more aggressive."

"More aggressive? What do you mean?"

"Make thyself noticed! You must get to know every prince, knight, and peasant you meet. Dress so they will notice you. Learn to catch their eyes at strategic moments and to giggle at their jokes. Thou art such a lovely girl; they shall fall for thee in no time. Behold and ye shall see."

"My father says I must guard my heart," the princess said.

"Guard thy heart for whom? You actually believe that a prince will come for you? Thou hast too much faith in thy father and his fairy tale dreams. You are sheltered here in this castle. Silly Princess, even if a prince were looking for you, he could not find you!"

"But what if he does come? My father says that my heart is the greatest gift I can give him."

"Hast thou not noticed, dear Princess, how many of thy friends mingle freely with the men in the courtyard, at the balls, and at the fairs? They are happy. Do you not see how much fun they are having?

They are enjoying life. Such friendships are harmless—in fact, they are healthy."

"Healthy?"

"Why, of course. Everyone knows that such relationships are necessary for one's education. How will you be able to know that Prince Charming is the one for you if you have never known anyone else? How will you get experience in socializing with knights? Think of the fun that you are missing—fun that you have every right to be enjoying!"

"Fun?" she asked. "I am not sure that I would classify it as such. After all, Maiden Flirtelia is heartbroken because the knight who said he was in love with her married Miss Peacock instead. Several of my other friends from the village are married ... but not happy."

"Go ahead then. Keep waiting. No one understands. No one ever will. You can live here in the castle forever with your parents. Keep waiting. It's fine with me. Never take any risks, never try anything new. Just stay where you are safe, and one by one watch your dreams perish and vanish away."

"There is a trouble far worse than never being married," declared the princess. "Being married to the wrong person. I much prefer to be happy and single than unhappily married. Marriage is not a right, but a gift."

At this the princess turned around and walked hastily inside the castle. She was tired of listening to his senseless words. Hoping to find a few minutes alone, she walked through the parlor, down the beautifully carved stone hall, and up the marble staircase to her bedroom. Closing the door behind her, she threw herself down onto her canopy bed and decided that she would not even try to hold back the tears that were already beginning to roll down her cheeks. Through her large western window, the evening sun rays were shining brightly into her room, illuminating the soft white rug and warming the feather quilt on which she was lying. But she was not enjoying the sunlight or taking any pleasure in the beauty of her royal quarters.

All at once, her pet canary began to sing cheerfully. The princess looked up at the pretty bird and wiped her tears away. When she opened the bronze cage, the little yellow bird jumped onto her hand

and continued his song. "I feel so lonely," the princess thought to herself. "I wish I could always be as happy as my bird is. He seems to be continually cheerful no matter of the circumstances."

With the canary perched on her shoulder, she turned toward the window, and peered at the distant mountains. Sighing deeply, she once again began to wonder if she would be single forever.

Despite her brave words to the alligator, the princess was not always so sure of her father's teaching when she was by herself. She never actually believed the alligator's words, but sometimes they did plant doubts in her mind. She subconsciously would believe little bits of his arguments, and because of the seed of Discontent growing in her heart, she was easily discouraged. As the days went by, she continued to dream of her future and struggle with her emotions. The more she felt sorry for herself, the more she looked out the window, and the more she looked out the window, the more the seed of Discontent grew.

But Waiting Is Hard

"I liked your talk on purity," a twelve-year-old young lady who had been in the audience said to me after my dad and I concluded a presentation called "Knights, Maidens, and Dragons."

"Oh, thank you," I said. "I think it's a really important topic."

"Yeah. My boyfriend and I have never kissed or anything."

"Oh … well … that's good. How long have you known him?"

She went on to tell me her story of how they met, how talented and good-looking he is, and what a perfect match they are.

"So is your boyfriend a Christian?" I asked.

"No, not yet, but I'm talking to him about it."

"Well, you know, the Bible teaches that it's wrong for a Christian to marry a non-Christian, so since it wouldn't be right for you to consider marrying him at this point, what is the purpose of developing a relationship with him?"

"Well, um … he's really nice, and … we're careful about what we do together."

"Let's see. You're twelve years old, right?"

"Right."

"When do you think would be the very soonest that you might get married?"

"Oh, maybe eighteen."

"That's six years away. Don't you think it would be better to focus on your walk with the Lord for right now and wait until you get closer to the age that you would consider marriage before developing a romantic relationship with someone?"

"But, Sarah, it's just so hard to wait!"

I *wanted* to say, "But you're *twelve* years old! Listen, you can wait! A lot of other people have had to wait a lot longer than you." But actually, I know that whether you're twelve or sixteen or thirty, it *is* hard to wait. In fact, waiting is one of the very hardest things God asks us to do.

The princess in our story is finding it difficult to wait, especially since she doesn't know how long she will have to keep waiting. What she doesn't realize is that this time of waiting is perhaps one of the most valuable times of her life. It is full of some of the richest lessons and greatest opportunities that she will ever experience.

Times of waiting take us to deeper levels of trust, strengthen our faith, remind us to abide in Christ, and teach us to delight in the Lord. There will be periods of waiting all through life, but for us as single young ladies, this season of life provides an ideal opportunity to learn the secret of being content in any situation (Phil. 4:11–13). If we can learn now how to patiently rest in the Lord, think how invaluable this "skill" will be throughout our entire lives.

WISHING FOR A LIFE WITHOUT STOPLIGHTS

Most people do not want to wait for anything. Think of all the devices people have developed to minimize waiting—microwaves, fast food, drive-thru's, credit cards, and e-mail, to name a few. These inventions may be convenient and helpful, but we will never escape seasons of waiting, because God knows how essential it is that we learn this quality. The Lord has different plans for each of us, but no matter who you are, God's plan for you includes stoplights. Think of the waiting that was required in the lives of Abraham, Sarah, Jacob, Joseph, Moses, David, Elizabeth, and others. In every one of their lives, waiting played an essential role in bringing about God's perfect plan. In fact, our entire life on earth is one of waiting—for God's promises, Christ's return, and our home in heaven (Heb. 11:13, Jn. 14:3, Rom. 8:23).

There are several consequences that occur when we fail to patiently wait for God to bring about His plans:

1. **We Miss God's Lessons.**

   God intends to teach us many things through seasons of waiting. We miss these special "classes" in perseverance, trust, and faith if we are not willing to wait. In fact, the Lord may even need to bring about more difficult trials to teach us the same lessons (Jas. 1:3–5).

2. **We Miss God's Best.**

   God desires to give us His very best. Many people have no idea what they missed, because they were not willing to wait to find out what the Lord had in store (Jer. 29:11).

3. **We Miss God's Help.**

   There are dangers that occur when we take matters into our own hands. The world still suffers today because of Abraham and Sarah's attempt to figure out their own solution to their problem of not having a son (Gal. 4:29). God wants us to learn to be dependent on Him. If we seek to "help" God accomplish what we think He should be doing, it always leads to trouble.

4. **We Miss God's Opportunities.**

   We miss the opportunity to show the world the power of God. When we by faith follow the ways of God, which the world considers foolish, others are able to see His sovereignty and love as they watch God work miraculously in the little details of our lives. Waiting is an opportunity to bring glory to His name and strengthen the faith of His people (Ex. 14:13–14).

PLEASE HURRY!

"How much longer, Dad?" I complained.

I was about thirteen years old, and Dad and I were late for a birthday party. I'd been looking forward to it all day, and now that it was time to go, Dad wasn't ready. At first I tried to wait patiently, but after waiting about half an hour, I was getting upset. After all, several families with girls my age were going to be at this party, and I was hoping to have as much time as possible to be with my friends!

"Dad, please hurry!" I whined. "We're already a half hour late, and I wanted to be *early*!"

Dad was still working on getting his present together, and he didn't seem to care that we were late. He didn't even seem to be hurrying. I was feeling annoyed.

"But Dad, I hate to be late!" I repeated.

"Mom," I begged, "will you please ask Dad to hurry up!"

After several more minutes of complaining on my part, Dad was finally ready to go. I jumped into the car, hoping Dad would drive fast! Approximately five minutes into our trip, Dad suddenly asked, "Did you bring the gift?"

"No, I thought you brought it."

"Well, I'd better turn around."

"But Dad, we're already really late!"

Needless to say, Dad turned around and we hurried home to pick up the forgotten gift. When we finally arrived at the party, Dad and I went to the door and found out that we were *early*! We had been mistaken about the time! In fact, we almost spoiled the surprise party by arriving too soon. It sure was a good thing that we were late!

In the same way, many times we may feel that our heavenly Father is slow in His working in our lives. We feel that He is late, and since He is taking so long, we think we'd better take matters into our own hands. But looking back, we always see that God is exactly on time. He is never a minute too late. If it is God's will for us to be married, then He will not leave us single for even one day longer than He knows is best, right, and perfect. But whenever we jump ahead of His timing, we find ourselves in an extremely dangerous position.

Over and over in my life I have found that God's timing is different than what I would have chosen. Often I think something needs to happen right away, but God doesn't seem to be in any hurry at all. In fact, He seems to purposely *want* me to be in positions where I have to wait. Looking back I understand. But looking forward isn't so easy.

ENTERING THE SPACE AGE

During the last eight or nine years, our family has been praying that the Lord would provide more space for our ministry. As Bright Lights and our family ministries have been growing, we have sensed an increasingly greater need for desks, computers, shelves, file cabinets, office space, meeting rooms, driveways, garages, and storage space.

Five years ago we thought it was the right time for God to provide this "ministry center," but nothing happened. Three years ago we really thought it was the right time. Our ministry kept expanding. I changed my bedroom into a Bright Lights office. I was sleeping downstairs in our basement, which had become a storage facility surrounded by walls built with boxes of books and Bright Lights notebooks. My parents had moved down there too, so at least I had company.

After another year or so had gone by, we thought, "Surely the Lord is going to provide something soon. We can't keep operating the way we are now." But we kept waiting, not wanting to act until the Lord provided the money and made it clear that He was directing us. We were committed to not going into debt. After all, God is able to provide without our help. Then about a year and a half ago I thought I had found the perfect place to set up an office for our ministry. Our whole family was excited! Finally, God is providing exactly what we need, I concluded. But then the Lord closed all the doors. I was disappointed and confused.

As our situation became more difficult, we continued to pray that the Lord would provide something—but what? We weren't even sure what to pray for. An office building? A bigger house? A pole barn out in the country?

Then, just last year the Lord supplied in a way we never would have expected! Through a very unusual (more than coincidental) chain of events, the Lord provided a second house for our family. It is bigger than our old one and has a large room in the basement that is perfect for gatherings. But the best feature of our new house is the location—it is directly behind our old one! Our family moved across the yard into our new home, and we turned our old house into a ministry center with offices, storage space, a resource room, a mail room, and a guest room.

The situation has been perfect. We have been able to be more efficient by having "work" in one place and "home" in another. Dad says that we've entered the space age. We have space to live, space to work, space for the helpers who come over, space for storage, space for cars, space for guests to stay, space for meetings, space for computers, space for bedrooms, and ... a nice courtyard between the two houses with a stone path from one back door to the other. Mom is very grateful to have a real bedroom again too!

Now we see that God's timing was right. Now we realize that we would not have been ready any sooner. But while you are in the season of waiting, it's hard to understand. Things don't make sense. It may feel as if God is absent. That's why it requires faith.

Fear or Faith?

There are two factors that will govern our decision making: fear and faith. Young ladies commonly struggle with many fears, especially in the area of marriage:

- What if I never get married?
- What if I have to wait until I'm thirty?
- How will I know God's will?
- What if everyone thinks I'm unpopular because I don't have a boyfriend?
- How will I know when I meet the right person?
- How will I know that it is the right time?
- What if I don't like the person God picks for me?

Did you know that many girls who live by fear have a boyfriend named Justin? His last name is Case. *Just in Case!* ☺

Fear is always counterproductive in our lives. Over and over in Scripture God gives the command to fear not. He has not given us the spirit of fear, but of power, of love, and of a sound mind (II Tim. 1:7). Our fears often cause us to make wrong choices. Many times fears are the driving force behind dating or other decisions, but we shouldn't be controlled by fear. We should be governed by faith.

Instead of Entertaining Fears:

- Refuse to listen to the lies Satan brings against you. Put into practice the things we discussed in the last chapter. Take captive wrong thoughts and replace them with Scripture. *"Resist the devil, and he will flee from you"* (Jas. 4:7).

- Remember that you are in a spiritual war, and use the weapons God has given you. *"Above all, taking the shield of faith, wherewith ye shall be able to quench all the fiery darts of the wicked"* (Eph. 6:16).

- Fear the Lord. All other fears diminish when you stay focused on living for the One who sees everything you do and to whom you will one day give account. *"Neither shall ye fear other gods. But the Lord your God ye shall fear; and He shall deliver you out of the hand of all your enemies"* (II Kgs. 17:38–39). *"In the fear of the Lord is strong confidence"* (Prov. 14:26).

- Pay attention to the needs of those around you, and purpose to lay down your life out of genuine love for the Lord and others. *"There is no fear in love; but perfect love casteth out fear"* (I Jn. 4:18).

- Meditate on specific verses that remind you to rest in the Lord. *"Be careful [anxious] for nothing; but in every thing by prayer and supplication with thanksgiving let your requests be made known unto God. And the peace of God, which passeth all understanding, shall keep your hearts and minds through Christ Jesus"* (Phil. 4:6–7).

- Know that when you fix your eyes on the Lord, there is no room for fear. *"Thou wilt keep him in perfect peace, whose mind is stayed on Thee: because he trusteth in Thee"* (Is. 26:3).

What Should I Do While I Wait?

Out of the corner of my eye I saw a lady walking up to me. I was standing in the front of a church that had invited our family to come and present several messages. She said, "I just wanted to take a minute, Sarah, to tell you not to become weary in well-doing. I know you are almost twenty-five years old, and I'm sure you've reached

Waste not thy youth only dreaming of a knight.

the age where you're wondering when you're going to get married. I just want to encourage you to press on in your ministry. Don't get discouraged. The enemy will attack, but don't listen to his fears. I'm sure you're not able to estimate just how important these single years are for ministry. Keep going!" She went on to tell me her story of the ministry God gave her during her single years and her testimony of how the Lord did not bring along the right husband for her until she was in her late thirties. "But it was His perfect time for me," she explained joyfully, "and I would never have been able to accomplish the same ministry if I had been married earlier."

This brings up an important point about waiting. You see, waiting doesn't mean just sitting around wondering when something is going to happen. Neither does it mean postponing marriage. Rather, it means serving the Lord faithfully right now wherever He has put you. If God keeps you single, He has work for you to do.

Waiting includes the idea of service. Think of a **wait**ress. Her job is to wait on tables—not to just sit around, but to serve, to make sure others' needs are met. This is the same concept communicated in the frequent command in Scripture to wait on the Lord. It doesn't mean we should do nothing. It means we should focus on Him and His work—serving God with all of our hearts, resting in Him, and trusting that He will take care of everything else. Waiting is patiently anticipating that which hasn't yet come and joyfully and diligently working on the Lord's business in the meantime.

BENEFITS OF WAITING ON THE LORD:

Here are some specific benefits that result from this kind of waiting on the Lord:

- You will not be ashamed (need not fear disappointment or disgrace, having confidence that God Himself is your ally).
  "For they shall not be ashamed that wait for Me" (Is. 49:23).
- The Lord will strengthen your heart.
  "Wait on the Lord: be of good courage, and He shall strengthen thine heart: wait, I say, on the Lord" (Ps. 27:14).
- You shall inherit the earth. (In the end, it is not the wicked who will receive lasting rewards, but the meek and humble.)
  "For evildoers shall be cut off: but those that wait upon the Lord, they shall inherit the earth" (Ps. 37:9).
- Your strength will be renewed.
  "But they that wait upon the Lord shall renew their strength; they shall mount up with wings as eagles; they shall run, and not be weary; and they shall walk, and not faint" (Is. 40:31).
- The Lord will be good to you.
  "The Lord is good unto them that wait for Him, to the soul that seeketh Him" (Lam. 3:25).

I've occasionally heard young ladies say something like this: "I wish I was a guy. They get to make all the decisions. They can just go and choose a wife. I mean, here is one of the biggest decisions in my life, and I can't do a thing about it! I just have to wait for someone to come to me!"

*Attempt not to assist **God** in the work that belongeth to **Him***

But think about that statement. Would you really want to make the decision yourself? Imagine the mess we could so easily get ourselves into. Aren't you grateful that we can let God handle it? Yes, we can pray, we can prepare, we can get to know people, we can be aware of those whom the Lord brings into our lives, we can discern godly young men, but we can't "cause" anything to happen. In fact, even if we date, we have no guarantee that we will ever get married. However, think of it this way: by putting us in a situation where we are powerless and unable to bring it about ourselves, we have no other good option but to trust the Lord. Faith is one of the most necessary aspects of the Christian life and God is giving us as single young ladies an ideal opportunity to learn and apply it. He wants us to be fully persuaded that He is more than able to take care of every need in our lives.

KEYS TO HELP YOU WAIT:

- Give up your own dreams and expectations. Actually, you don't have to give them up; but rather, exchange them. Exchange your dreams for something far better—God's perfect plan. Choose to will what God wills (Mt. 10:39).

- Stop. Be still and know that He is God. Consider the awesome power of the God that you serve. What seems impossible to you is nothing for Him. Be still and watch Him work (Ps. 46:10).
- Get out a sheet of paper and begin to list the benefits that you are experiencing through this time of waiting. Don't just make a list in your head. It is helpful to actually write out the benefits. Don't stop until you have at least ten benefits on your list.
- Rejoice in this time of waiting. I know it is hard. It's hard for me too. As I mentioned, waiting is one of the most difficult things God asks us to do. Sometimes it feels like you just can't wait any longer. But struggles and trials are important parts of our lives. Scripture commands us to rejoice in these times of trials (Jas. 1:2, I Pet. 4:12–13).
- Redirect your focus. Don't focus on the *waiting*; focus on the Lord.
- In the little events of daily life, learn to look to the Lord to supply your needs and carry your burdens. Have the attitude of David who prayed, *"On Thee do I wait all the day ... My soul, wait thou only upon God; for my expectation is from Him"* (Ps. 25:5, 62:5).

THREE IMPATIENT CHILDREN

"When is Daddy coming home?" Susie asked.

"I don't know," answered Zach, "but I sure hope he comes soon."

"Maybe we should just start without him," Jordan said.

"He told us to wait," Susie insisted.

"Yes, but maybe he didn't know that he'd be gone this long," commented Zach.

"We'll just shoot off a couple of the fireworks," Jordan decided, "but we'll save most of them for when Dad gets home."

With excitement, the three children took out a brightly colored firecracker from the brown paper bag that their father had given them.

"Now step back, everyone," Jordan exclaimed as he set the firecracker on the ground, lit the wick, and then jumped back.

Boy, were those three children in for a surprise! They had not read the package and didn't realize that they had lit a fountain instead of a rocket. They also had left their brown bag of fireworks much too close, and soon the entire bag caught on fire. In one short, spectacular moment, all the fireworks went off at once.

Just then their father came running around the house to find out what was happening. After making sure everyone was okay, he picked up the remains of the bag and began asking questions.

"I'm sorry," he said as he looked through the pieces, "but they are all used up. Why didn't you wait for me?"

Susie started to cry. "You mean, we don't get to see the fireworks show?" she asked sorrowfully.

Their father had planned something special for them, but they had ruined it by attempting to carry it out themselves. Jordan, Zach, and Susie learned the hard way that when you are not willing to wait, you face *danger* now and miss the *joy* later. [1]

Waiting is hard. But it's necessary. It only makes the final outcome better and sweeter. And it teaches many valuable lessons along the way. Ask the Lord for help. He will always give us the strength to do what He has called us to do.

SUGGESTED MEMORY VERSE:

"For the Lord God is a sun and shield: the Lord will give grace and glory: no good thing will He withhold from them that walk uprightly. O Lord of hosts, blessed is the man that trusteth in Thee" (Psalm 84:11–12).

SUGGESTED ASSIGNMENT:

During seasons of waiting, it is especially important that we learn to focus on the needs of other people rather than on our own needs.

---

1   Adapted from Arthur S. Maxwell, *Uncle Arthur's Bedtime Stories*, Review and Herald Publishing Association. Used by permission.

Ask the Lord to bring to mind one person whom you can encourage (perhaps a brother, a sister, or a young lady you know). Begin to look for ways to minister to and uplift this person—and ultimately to instruct him or her in the ways of the Lord. Think of some practical ways that you can begin to invest in his or her life this week, such as by writing notes of encouragement, spending some one-on-one time together, reading the Bible together, sharing lessons from your life, calling this person on the phone, making a small gift, or maybe even meeting on a weekly basis in order to disciple this individual.

Jesus says, *"He that is faithful in that which is least is faithful also in much"* (Lk. 16:10). As we are faithful to obey the Lord in the "little" assignments He gives, He then opens bigger and greater opportunities for service.

CHAPTER SEVEN

How Parents Can Help

*"My son, give me thine heart, and let thine
eyes observe my ways."*
Proverbs 23:26

The sun was shining brightly and the May flowers were beginning to blossom, but the princess did not seem to notice or to care. She had tears in her eyes, and her thoughts were elsewhere.

"What is wrong, my daughter?" her father asked.

"Oh nothing, I just ... oh, if only a knight would come and rescue me in my distress."

"Distress? What peril hath befallen thee, my dearest daughter?"

"Oh, my father, I be not betrothed. No great knight has sought my hand. Thy daughter becometh an old maid!"

"And you are not happy?" questioned the king, looking at her intently.

"Well, sometimes I am, but—"

"Until thou learnest to be content in the place God has put you, you will never be happy or fulfilled anywhere. Do not forget, my daughter, that your years have been useful. You have accomplished much. Your bright light has reached to many."

"But how long will I have to wait?" The princess sighed and sat down on a bench in the courtyard.

"If your heavenly Father told you, then it would not require any faith on your part," the king commented. "You would not learn the lessons or gain the rewards that directly result from waiting."

"Yes, I suppose. But I hope my time of waiting is almost over ... Oh, Father, I have been meaning to ask you something," said the princess, standing up again. "Remember that time we talked about the Spring Fair? You said it was permissible for me to go, but explained how I must be a candle and a rose."

"Yes, I remember. You met Sir Eloquence there," replied the king.

"Um, yes," she said, not wanting to be reminded of him. Then she continued with her question. "I was wondering, thinkest thou that I should attend the Merchants' Fest in Carnalville? I realize it is not the manner of event of which we approve—"

"The Merchants' Fest?" he asked in surprise.

"I know thou hast said that it is dangerous and just a foolish party. I know there will be much dancing and evil talk, but I will be careful to stay away from any wicked company. I understand that I do not need to try to search for a husband, but Father, do you not think that I at least need to be meeting more young men? After all, I am nearly twenty-one."

"You do not know what you ask. It is when thy heart is longing so, and thy faith wavering, that thou art in the greatest danger."

"But, Father, I fear not!" the princess declared.

"Yea, therefore I fear!" her father answered.

"Father, you seem to be so worried about everything!"

"The prudent man foreseeth the evil, and hideth himself: but the simple pass on and are punished," recited the king.

"The alligator speaks of the festivities and the social banquets to be enjoyed," she continued.

"The **alligator** eats the scum at the bottom of the moat," the king added dryly.

"The other maidens will all be going, and I will stay with them," explained the princess as she began to wander slowly through the courtyard. "They mingle oft with the young men in the village. The alligator says that such relationships are healthy."

"But thou are forgetting that thou art a princess," said her father, following her. "Remember thou also that the alligator hath dragon's blood in his veins."

"But, others—"

"Others do not understand that a little foolishness ruins the testimony of one who has wisdom and honor."

"But others—"

"Others do not have me as their father. Others do not represent the royal family."

"But **everyone** is going to the Merchants' Fest!"

"When you chose to follow the way of purity, did you expect it to be easy? When you decided to wait for the best, did you think that waiting would be fun? Did you think that your faith would not be tested? When you decided to take the narrow path, did no one warn you that difficulties, hardship, and tears would be part of the journey, and that you would often face rejection from others and be forced to walk alone? My daughter, that which you wait for the longest you treasure the most, and through much struggle the prize is won."

Her father turned and walked slowly into the palace, leaving the princess to think by herself. The tears were just starting again as she continued her way outside the castle. She leaned against the edge of the bridge and watched a few ducks swim by. As I'm sure you can guess, the silence lasted only a minute, for the tears rolling down her cheeks and into the moat below attracted the attention of her persistent friend, the alligator.

"So, you finally are realizing that your plans are failing. Well, it is about time thou camest to thy senses," said the alligator.

"I do not wish to talk," she replied, wiping the tears from her cheeks.

"Ahh, but you do. You want to tell your whole life story to someone who wants to hear every detail, to someone who loves and admires you, to someone who holds you close, to—"

"Well, alright, but I do not want to talk to you."

"You need not. Just listen. For I believe that now is the time to reconsider your ways and to allow yourself to grow up. Thou hast no reason to cry. The Merchants' Fest is but one week away."

"My father does not want me to go."

"But he never actually said that you could not go. I was listening myself."

"Perhaps he would allow it. But he does not want me to. He says it would not be wise."

"But Princess, you are a woman, not a little child. You need not follow every little suggestion from thy father."

"No, I need not. But up to this point, I have always found the counsel of my parents to be valuable. Their caution in the past has not been unwarranted. Should I forsake now that which has guided me for so long?"

"Get out of the nest where you are so comfortable and explore the new and the different," the alligator persisted. *"You can be careful in Carnalville. That's all your father really meant, anyway."*

"No, that is not all he meant. He meant much, much more."

"So what will you do, silly Princess? Stay here and wait for a handsome knight to appear?"

"I know not. Please let me be by myself!"

A Special Provision From God

In the world in which we live, is it even possible to enter into marriage pure and free from scars? After all, we are surrounded by every kind of temptation and polluting influence, and we have an enemy prowling around like a roaring lion who is doing everything he can to destroy godly marriages. Well, because of these dangers, and because this project of finding a life partner is so important—not only for our lives, but also for the future generations to come—the Lord has given us some much-needed support to help us along the way. He knows that we wouldn't be able to make it on our own, so He has provided some extra special assistance to guide us through, to give us wisdom, to protect us, and to help in any way we need it. This special provision is our parents. Unfortunately, we as human beings seem to be rather skilled at rejecting God's most valuable gifts.

A little girl named Julia who lived on the mission field with her parents suddenly became ill with a fever. Her mother knew exactly what was wrong, and she had some medicine that would help. She brought this medicine to her daughter, who was lying sick in bed, and insisted that she take it immediately. With disgust, Julia complained that the medicine tasted horrible. She refused to even look at it. Her mother became stern, saying that if she did not take it, she would get seriously ill and could even die. Still, Julia refused. Mother began to plead with her sick daughter to take the medicine. Finally, Julia agreed that if her mother left the room, she would swallow the disgusting syrup.

With a sigh of relief, her mother left, and upon her return a few minutes later, she was delighted to see that the bottle of precious medicine stood empty. Her mother was confident that Julia would soon recover, but during the night her fever crept very high. All night long her mother sat by her bed trying to keep the fever down. Finally, in the morning, poor Julia confessed with tears that she had not taken the medicine at all; instead, she had thrown it out the window. Her disobedience had nearly cost her her life. [1]

Just as Julia refused the good gift her mother wanted to give her, so we often reject the good gifts God wants to give us. Most people, in fact, reject His greatest gift of all—eternal life. Imagine being unwilling to accept a gift so unspeakably wonderful!

This is exactly the same way we tend to act when it comes to God's provision of parents. Over and over, Proverbs reminds us of the value of listening to our parents' instruction. Parents are a gift from the Lord. Yet often we, as Julia, reject the very thing that God intends for our happiness, good, and protection.

The young lady who is committed to God's best and desires to establish safeguards in her life will realize the tremendous protection

---

1   Adapted from Arthur S. Maxwell, *Uncle Arthur's Bedtime Stories*, Review and Herald Publishing Association. Used by permission.

the Lord has given her through her parents. God is the One who has set in place all human authority, and He works through it to accomplish His good purposes in each of our lives (Rom. 13:1, Eph. 6:2–3).

IMPERFECT PARENTS

Some of you who are reading this may not have Christian parents or may not have parents to guide you at all, so I want to be quick to mention that God will always be faithful to provide the help you need. Be assured that even though your parents make mistakes, our heavenly Father *never* makes mistakes, and He has given you exactly the right parents for you. He will use them for good as He works out His perfect plan in your life. If you do not have parents, remember that the Lord Himself becomes a special Father to those who do not have an earthly one (Ps. 68:5). If your parents are not Christians, understand that the Lord can still work through them. Of course, if they give you counsel that conflicts with clear teaching from God's Word (such as encouraging you to marry an unbeliever), you should obey the Bible, no matter what the consequences might be. But often the Lord will give good direction and protection even through unbelieving authorities. It could be that God is doing two things at once. Maybe it isn't that He gave *you* unsaved parents, but that He gave *them* a Christian daughter. He cares for them, too, and your obedience is His tool in their lives. We do not know all that God is doing, but if we love Him and apply ourselves to His purposes, He works out all things together for our good (Rom. 8:28). When needed, He will also bring you help through other sources—perhaps through your pastor or a godly older couple at your church. It is our responsibility to accept and appreciate the protection and assistance the Lord gives.

For most of us, however, this special help we need will be provided through our parents. This doesn't mean that parents make all the decisions, but it is noteworthy to recognize that in Biblical times parents were often involved in choosing their children's mates, and fathers were held responsible for their daughters' purity (Gen. 24, 28:1–2, Ex. 34:16, Dt. 7:1–4).

The first time I remember discussing the topic of marriage with my mom was when I was very little. I can't recall exactly what she said, but I remember that I had the impression that *my dad* was going to pick out *my husband*. That sounded fine to me. In fact, I liked the idea. ☺ A few years later while in class at my Christian school, my teacher explained that parents in Bible times would choose mates for their children. I raised my hand and enthusiastically told the class, "In our family, we're going to do that too!" Needless to say, my classmates were surprised. One girl asked in disbelief, "Sarah, you are actually going to let *your dad* pick out your husband?"

Despite the comments from these friends, I wasn't worried at all. I knew that our family was going to be like a team working on this together. I didn't know how the Lord was going to bring my future husband to me (I still don't know ☺), but I knew that I could trust the Lord to work through my authorities.

Don't panic, anyone! I'm not talking about arranged marriages. Our parents love us and they want what's best for us. My parents would never, ever dream of forcing me to marry someone I didn't want to marry. In the same way, I would never want to marry someone without my parents' input and blessing. You see, if we understand that God works through our parents, then we will realize that parental involvement is not something to be scared of, but rather to be thankful for. I'm sure you would agree that getting married is one of the most important decisions we will ever make—much more important than whether or not we go to college, what interests we pursue, or where we live. We should be grateful for our parents' protection and willingness to be involved. Our parents know us better than anyone else does, and they desire the very best for our lives. Not only this, but our parents have more experience and understanding than we do. We should take their advice seriously!

SEVEN REASONS TO SEND YOUNG MEN TO YOUR DAD

Whenever I talk to young ladies about this topic, I like to encourage them to make a commitment to direct any young men who express interest in them to their dads first. If you make this commitment now and tell your father, it can have many benefits.

1. Your father will respect you and know he can trust you.
2. You and your dad will be a team working on this together.

If thou wouldest marry the princess,
thou must first petition the king.

3. The young man will respect you. Even if he is surprised and finds this to be a completely new concept, he will still respect your conviction.
4. If the young man won't go ask your father, then you know he's not the one for you. It's a good way to screen guys.
5. If you aren't interested in a persistent young man, well, you can let your dad explain that to him—makes it easier for you! ☺
6. If he *does* go talk to your father, your dad will probably see things in this young man's life that you do not see. He will be able to give you caution, wisdom, and guidance.
7. If this *is* the right young man for you, he and your dad will start off their relationship on the right foot. From the beginning they will respect each other and have good fellowship. This is going to be an important relationship in the years to come.

"Dad," Laura exclaimed as she returned home from a Bright Lights meeting, "when I get older, you don't have to worry about me and boys, because I'm gonna send any boys who are interested in me to you." Her dad was a little surprised—especially since he had always imagined that when his girls became teenagers, he'd have Jeeps outside his house honking as he watched his daughters run out the door to take off with their boyfriends. This father was, therefore, definitely happy to hear about the decision his eleven-year-old daughter had made that evening. He was also a little worried about how he would handle this new responsibility that had been thrust on his shoulders!

My friend Laura is twenty now and one of the Bright Lights leaders. Today she says how thankful she is for this decision, which has significantly protected her. You see, Laura's decision when she was eleven was more than just a choice to not date. It was a commitment to stay under her dad's protection and to guard her heart, trusting it with her father until the day when she would get married.

It is important at the start of every marriage that the parents of both the bride and of the groom give their blessing on it. A very wise commitment to make is that you will not marry someone unless both sets of parents are in favor of it and extend their full blessing. This is a key safeguard that God has put in place.

What happens if a young man and a young woman are interested in each other, but one or more of the parents is against the marriage? Well, remember that just because the parents say no *now* doesn't mean it could never happen later. If it is of God, He can bring it to pass. God is the One who gave these parents to these young people. Maybe the parents can tell it is not the right time yet. Maybe they see that more maturity is needed on the part of one or both of the young people. Nevertheless, the Lord is the One in control, and He is able to work through the authorities He has set in place.

Don't Keep Secrets

"I've been doing some stupid things, Sarah," Crystal acknowledged. "I'd like to talk with you."

Crystal was a girl I'd known for about six years. She was a sweet friend with a gracious personality and a heart for the Lord. But, just like all of us, I knew that Crystal was having some struggles.

"Okay, let's talk. It's lunchtime. Wanna find a place to eat?"

"Sure. Sounds good."

After talking about all the possible restaurants we passed, we ended up at our favorite bagel shop—the one where I always seem to end up at—but only after an extensive discussion of all the other restaurants in town and an "I don't care. You pick. No, I don't care. You pick." interchange.

After getting through the small talk, ordering our lunches, and catching up on news, we finally reached the real subject matter.

"Well, Sarah," Crystal began, "Adam has liked me for a while now. At first I insisted that I was not interested in him. I knew he didn't have the character traits I was looking for in a husband … but I still wanted to be friends with him. Since I didn't have very many friends in the area, I soon found myself really appreciating his companionship. My parents warned me to be careful. Years ago I made the decision to guard my heart and save it for one man. I knew all along that I didn't want to get too attached to Adam, but it's not like I was dating him or anything! We were just friends—that's all. At least that's all that it was supposed to be. But during the past few months, my relationship with my parents has been really hard, and I feel like they are always critical of me and telling me what to do. This has just caused me to get closer to Adam. As a result, my parents have been giving me more and more cautions in regard to our friendship. They specifically told me that I shouldn't be e-mailing him. But over the past few months I've been so lonely, I've started writing back and forth to Adam, text messaging, and talking occasionally on the phone."

"And your parents don't know?"

Crystal slowly shook her head and answered, "Not everything."

"Well, I hate to tell you what you already know," I began …

"That's okay," she sighed.

"Well, first off, make sure that you call things what they are," I said slowly. "You mentioned a number of times that you've done some 'stupid' things. I know what you mean, but be careful to call sin 'sin.' Deceitfulness with parents is not something to take lightly, and as soon as the enemy gets us to compromise in one area, it opens doors for further temptation."

"Yeah, I know. I need to have a talk with Mom and Dad."

"Soon," I said as I nodded and smiled. "And as you obey the Lord in this area, He will direct your paths and lead you in other areas as well. I know you feel unsure about what the Lord has ahead for you, but you can't expect Him to direct and increase your ministry if you aren't obedient in what He has already asked you to do."

We discussed the whole situation and talked about guarding our hearts, but most of all I encouraged Crystal that the first thing she needed to do was to confess her disobedience to her parents and tell them the whole story. I appreciated Crystal's humble response and obvious desire to do what was right. I promised to pray for her.

About a week later I received a call.

"Crystal? Hi! How are you?"

"Oh, I'm so much more encouraged than I've been for a long time," she answered enthusiastically. "Sarah, well, I had that talk I needed to have with my parents. Sunday afternoon I asked them if we had time for a serious talk. I wasn't sure whether to hope that they'd say yes or no, but they told me it would be a good time. It was hard, Sarah. It was really hard. I confessed everything and we talked for several hours. I wished I could just type a letter to them, because it's easier to type than talk when you're holding back tears at the same time … but I knew that in person would be better. And you know, if you had told me a week ago that if I had this miserable talk with my parents I'd feel great and everything would be lots better, I would never have believed you. But, it's true! This week things have improved so much. My relationship with my parents is less strained, and they have been talking with Adam and giving me clear direction regarding our relationship. Adam's growing spiritually … I'm growing spiritually … I feel such a freedom—and I'm just so encouraged!"

EMBRACE THE SAFEGUARD

One of the most important commitments I ever made was that I would not keep any secrets from my parents. If there are any areas in your life that your parents do not know about, particularly any "little" areas of deceitfulness, then I'd encourage you to follow Crystal's example and tell them everything. Yes, *everything*.

I understand how difficult it is to humble yourself, especially if you feel that your parents have also been wrong. But remember, the Lord exalts those who humble themselves. It's a promise. (See James 4:10.) So take the most humble road possible. Have a talk with your parents. Don't bring up any of your claims against them. Don't defend yourself. Just take the blame and ask forgiveness. You will find the same rewards that Crystal found.

A second lesson to learn from Crystal's story is the importance of listening to the advice of your parents. Many times my parents have recognized cautions that I have not discerned. It takes faith to listen to your parents' wisdom when you don't understand. It's hard. It's tempting to just rationalize that you know better in this situation. It's difficult to submit. But time after time, I have seen how God has used my parents for good.

I have seen the Lord richly bless those young ladies I know who have chosen to honor their fathers. Ephesians 5 commands husbands to love their wives, and wives to respect their husbands. As women desire to be loved, so men desire to be respected. In order to be prepared to respect and submit to a future husband, it is crucial that we learn now to honor our fathers. Ask the Lord to strengthen your relationship with your dad and to give you ideas about how you can honor him in your daily life.

My friend Olivia recently shared with me that the Lord has been challenging her to look for little ways to honor and bless her father each day. One afternoon a few weeks ago she was planning to throw together a quick supper for her dad and then spend the rest of the day doing what *she* wanted to do. But then the Lord reminded her of the choice she had made to strive to serve and respect her father in the little things. Instead of making the quick supper that she knew was not her dad's favorite meal, she decided to ask him what he would especially like her to make. She chose to forfeit her time and schedule in order to do something special for him.

It takes effort to serve, submit, and communicate with your father, but God promises blessings for those who do. In addition, it will be very meaningful to your dad and important preparation for your future marriage. Speak well of your father to others. Pray for him every day. Ask him to give you direction in ministry. Express gratefulness for the things he does for you. This attitude of honor is greatly pleasing in God's sight (I Pet. 3:4–6).

One evening while teaching a Bright Lights meeting on the topic of polluting influences, I challenged the girls in my group to make a commitment to listen to their fathers' words of protection. I gave them a certificate to sign and then take home for their father to sign also:

This certifies that I have made it my goal to stay under my father's protection.

Thank you for praying for God's protection over me.

Thank you also for protecting me from polluting influences, evil material, worldly thinking, wrong friends, and anything that causes wrong thoughts, words, and actions.

I will strive to follow your guidance regarding these influences and keep myself from being polluted by the world.

Daughter's Signature: _____

Father's Signature: _____

One girl enthusiastically showed her father this certificate, asked him to sign it, and put it in her Bright Lights notebook. Several years later as this young lady was excitedly talking about an activity she was looking forward to, her father interrupted her and said, "I don't want you to be involved in that activity."

"But, Dad," she complained, "this is something I really want to do."

"I'm sorry," her dad explained, "but I think this particular activity is going to hinder your spiritual walk, produce wrong thoughts, and distract you from the Lord."

"Dad," she persisted, "I won't let it affect me in that way. There's nothing wrong with it. And besides, many of my strong Christian friends are doing it."

Finally her dad responded, "Do you remember several years ago when you asked me to sign a certificate to protect you from polluting influences? Well, I am trying to fulfill my responsibility of protecting you."

She listened to her father, and even though she was very disappointed, she decided not to participate in this particular activity. Now, several years later, this young lady has told me how grateful she is for her father's protection in this area. She agrees that this activity would not have been wise, and looking back she is able to clearly see that the Lord worked through her father for good.

"He is in the way of life that keepeth instruction" (Prov. 10:17). *"My son, keep thy father's commandment, and forsake not the law of thy mother"* (Prov. 6:20).

Wise knights kill not dragons single-handedly.

Obstacles to Parental Involvement

I hope you are beginning to see that parental involvement is a good thing, something to be grateful for, and a valuable gift from God. Of course, it is not always easy to humbly receive it. The enemy will work hard to keep us from the blessings found in working together with our parents. Here are two difficult obstacles he places in our way:

1. Damaged Relationships

Satan seeks to destroy our relationship with our parents by stirring up bitterness, anger, and rebellion. Obviously, this will be a huge hindrance to the strong, healthy, working relationship that is needed in order for parents and children to be able to freely discuss important topics like marriage. That is why it's essential to clear up any past offenses and to work on being close to our parents now.

2. Cultural Influence

The world is working *against* us. The world is telling us to do things the opposite of the Biblical way, to be independent from our parents, and to make our own decisions. Therefore, we must realize that this is just another area in which we as Christians need to be willing to stand alone by following God's way and honoring our parents.

BENEFITS TO PARENTAL INVOLVEMENT

1. Wisdom and caution from someone older and wiser—who loves you and has your very best interests in mind
2. Valuable insight in evaluating a young man's character
3. Help in protecting emotions
4. Caution when you're headed in a wrong direction or not aware of danger
5. Accountability
6. Help in discerning the right steps and the right timing
7. Freedom that comes from knowing that God will work through earthly authorities

A godly twenty-five-year-old man fell in love with a young lady named Maria who was twenty years old. They were both mature Christians committed to using their lives for the Lord's work. In fact, both were already missionaries, and they met on the mission field. It seemed like a perfect match—except for one problem. Maria's parents had died many years earlier, and she had been working with an elderly lady who was a fellow missionary. Surprisingly, this lady was completely opposed to their marriage and began to spread false rumors about the young man. She would not allow him to have any contact with Maria.

The two young people were heartbroken and grieved, and wondered what they should do. Believing that God would work through the authorities set in place, this young man wrote a letter to Maria's uncle (her legal guardian) to request her hand in marriage. It seemed like an impossible situation. The elderly lady also wrote letters to the uncle and other relatives trying to discredit the young man's reputation. The uncle had never even met the young man—surely he would believe the lies. But the young people trusted that the Lord would work through authorities. Four long and difficult months went by as they waited for a response from the uncle. At last, a letter arrived! Maria's uncle had researched the situation himself, and to their utter joy and amazement, he had granted permission for the marriage.

This young man was Hudson Taylor, a well known missionary to China. He and Maria Dyer were blessed with a very happy marriage. Later he wrote, "I have never known disobedience to the definite command of a parent, even if that parent were mistaken, that was not followed by retribution. Conquer through the Lord. He can open any door."

Shortly after their marriage, Hudson Taylor said, "Oh, to be married to the one you do love, and love most tenderly and devotedly ... that is bliss beyond the power of words to express or imagination conceive. There is no disappointment *there*. And every day as it shows more of the mind of your Beloved, when you have such a treasure as mine, makes you only more proud, more happy, more humbly thankful to the Giver of all good for this best of earthly gifts." Their story is a beautiful example of how God desires to bless those who honor their authorities and trust in His timing.

SUGGESTED MEMORY VERSE:

"My son, give me thine heart, and let thine eyes observe my ways" (Proverbs 23:26).

SUGGESTED ASSIGNMENT:

In chapter one, we discussed how a true princess does not simply tolerate safeguards—she embraces them. One way to demonstrate your desire to embrace your parents' protection would be to make your own certificate similar to the one mentioned in this chapter. Sign it, present it to your father (and/or mother), and ask him to sign it as well. Keep it in a place where it will be a reminder to both of you of your commitment.

The Great Toboggan Ride

TESTIMONY BY MY SISTER GRACE

"Come on, you guys!" I called to my friends at the top of the sledding hill. "If we get a lot of people on this toboggan it will go really fast!" It was the first big snowfall of the year. The hill was packed. I had arranged for a group from our church to go sledding together, and I was delighted when I saw that one of my friends had brought a toboggan. *This is going to be fun,* I thought as I took the front seat and four of my friends piled on behind me.

As we were about ready for the push off, my dad approached the scene.

"Wait! You can't go down on that!" he said. "That's really dangerous!"

Oh great, why does Dad always have to get involved and spoil the fun? I thought. Feeling slightly embarrassed by his cautiousness, I told Dad that we would be fine.

"No," he insisted. "Look down there. There are tons of little kids. You could hit any one of them! It could be a serious accident."

Oh brother, everyone knows that sledding involves a little risk, but it always turns out fine, I thought.

"This toboggan is like a killer machine going down the mountain!" Dad continued. "Someone could die!"

"Dad," I explained, "This is what sledding *is*. People know to move out of the way."

"That's false! It will be going too fast. The hill is crowded. I don't think you should go down!"

By now the whole church party was listening and wondering what would happen. My friends on the toboggan all thought it would be fine. Sarah thought it was fine. I thought it was fine. Even the other adults didn't seem very worried, so finally my dad reluctantly backed off, and we started down the hill.

"We'll just yell really loudly so people will get out of our way," we told my dad.

Down we went. We got going faster and faster and it was really fun—until—we hit a little six-year-old girl. She went flying and did a complete flip over the top of the toboggan.

We came to a stop, jumped off, and ran back to the girl who was now standing up and in her dad's arms. "Is she okay?" my friend asked.

"Well, what do *you* think?" her dad snapped back. It was obvious that he was very upset. *Why did this have to happen the one time my dad cautioned us not to go?* I wondered.

It turned out that the little girl seemed fine, just shook up. Then a disturbing thought came to me: *Dad is at the top of the hill and saw all of this happen.*

Yes, Dad had endured several seconds of sheer horror from the top of the hill as he watched the little girl fly through the air. I returned to him right away, feeling repentant and concerned, and we discussed what to do. We looked for the little girl and her family but they had already left.

The sledding party had suddenly become much more sober. All the other people from my church had watched me disregard my dad's caution and then end up in this trouble. We all learned a lesson. I asked my dad to forgive me, and I was very grateful to the Lord that it didn't turn out any worse.

A few weeks later … on Christmas morning, I noticed that there was a gift from Dad standing up behind the tree. I smiled when I saw that it was a sparkly-red miniature toboggan. Next to it there was a poem entitled "The Great Toboggan Ride." The poem explained how in life there are a lot of different "toboggans"—things that seem fun for a while but then lead to trouble.

A "toboggan ride" could be a relationship with a boyfriend, the immoral atmosphere of a secular college or high school, or participation with friends who pull you in a wrong direction. It could also be reading romance novels, watching television and movies, listening to rock music, telling lies, or being careless in our Internet activity.

Satan, who knows our weaknesses, will use different temptations in each of our lives. Toboggans always go in one direction. Down. It's a slippery slope. We get going faster and faster and it's hard to stop! Toboggans are difficult to control. We may hop on because our friends are all doing it, but soon we see that we are going to crash. Even if we jump off mid-flight, it's a climb to get back to where we were. It seems so easy just to get on a toboggan and slide down, and so hard to climb upward to God's best. But the small amount of fun that we may have going down on the toboggan doesn't even compare to the peace, the joy, and the reward that God gives when we follow His way and climb to earn the prize. We need to be going up, not down!

Before You Meet Prince Charming

CHAPTER EIGHT

Have a Life Purpose Bigger than Marriage

"But seek ye first the kingdom of God, and His righteousness; and all these things shall be added unto you."
Matthew 6:33

*S*o, you decided not to go to the Merchants' Fest?" the alligator sneered as soon as he had a chance to talk with the princess. "Once again thou hast listened to thy father's old-fashioned ideas. Much as I try to help you out, you just never are willing to listen. I am beginning to feel that thy situation is hopeless. Thou wilt be eighty years old and still sitting here dreaming of Prince Charming."

"I am not listening to thee, Mr. Alligator," she answered. "I will not be governed by fear, no matter how many fiery darts you thrust at me."

"So, you are getting feisty, are you? Thou makest me laugh.

And what, I ask, will you do since you are not joining the Fest in Carnalville? Sit here and cry, I suppose?"

"I do not know," the princess sighed.

"That is thy very problem, dearest daughter," said her father, stepping onto the west balcony. "I could not help but overhear thy conversation. If thy life is not filled with what is most important, thou wilt fall into despair and self-pity. Take courage, daughter. Thou art doing well. You may have only a short time of singleness left. Use it wisely. As they say, do not doubt in the darkness what thou hast believed in the light. The work you are doing is just as important as the work of the bravest knights in the kingdom. You use not a sword of metal, but one of gentle words and helpful hands. Lift up a banner of truth and conviction. It will attract the young ladies of honor. They are thy work. Thou trainest the young ladies of the kingdom, the future mothers and wives—the heart, beauty, and soul of the kingdom. Continue, I charge thee, to fight the good fight. Do not give up when the way is hard. Persevere, my daughter, and never forget the One who is a rewarder of all who seek Him."

"All the kingdom should hear thy speech, my father," the princess said, smiling at him. "Yes, I will try to do as you say. It truly is my desire. And, Mr. Alligator, I am not afraid of thy foolish threats or—"

But the alligator was no longer in sight, for he always seemed to disappear when the king was nearby.

A moment later one of the king's servants stepped out onto the balcony and bowed to the king.

"Your Highness," the servant began, "I am sorry to interrupt, but there is a knight outside the court who requests to see thee."

"Yes, yes, I'll be happy to visit with him. I will meet him in a short while. Escort him into the Great Hall."

The king gave a loving hug to the princess and then stepped inside. He followed the winding staircase down to the armory and entered the west wing of the Great Hall.

"My lord, the king," spoke Sir Valiant respectfully, greeting the king on bended knee.

"Sir Valiant! Rise, trusted knight. How fare thee? It is good to see you. And what business brings thee to the castle?"

"Greetings, Your Majesty. I fare well. I trust Your Highness is in good health. I come seeking thy mind on a matter of considerable concern regarding the security of the kingdom."

"Speak on, Sir Valiant. Be there a threat of war? A new enemy?"

"It is not new to thee, Sire. It is as old as the kingdom itself, but it raises its head anew in every generation."

The king listened with interest as Valiant continued. "There be two enemies invading the land—a dragon and a giant. But no ordinary dragon and no ordinary giant. I am confident that the king has been aware of them always. As thou knowest, they be invisible but do great damage."

"Of which dragon and giant dost thou speak?" questioned the king.

"The dragon called Lies and the giant named Temptation. The dragon's very breath be venomous. He lurks from village to village in the darkness, poisoning people with his deceptions. Some get eaten

alive. Believing his words, they are straightway snatched in one bite between his sharp teeth. Others are not immediately taken in; nevertheless, sooner or later, because they do not resist him, they are squeezed in the coil of his tail. Many a village hath been set ablaze by his fiery words—coming from the very flames of hell. They kindle false concepts in house after house, and as these spread through the village they be leaving whole families unprotected."

"If the foundations be destroyed, what can the righteous do?" said the king, quoting the eleventh Psalm.

"The giant likewise is ruining entire towns with his lusts," said Sir Valiant. "He stirs up men's appetites during the day, and in the evening he swings his club. It is a magical weapon that appears not as a club but as many forms of enticing attractions. At first they are

painless, but soon they bring grief, bitterness, guilt, and destruction. My lord, I have fought many enemies, but these are formidable indeed. I have come to seek thy counsel."

The king paced back and forth a couple of times while deep in thought and then spoke. "When the enemy attacks with force, a banner must be lifted up. A standard of truth, a banner of righteousness, a flag calling men to action. A standard to mobilize the men of conviction, the men of God."

"The dragon will flee if resisted," the king declared, speaking with confidence and authority. "He cannot face truth. And the giant loves darkness; he will retreat from the light. One of honor and bravery must raise this standard, and the honorable and brave men of the kingdom will rise to the battle."

"Thy counsel is good, Sire," said Valiant. "The truth must be proclaimed. Leaders must be trained."

"Sir Valiant, thou art a faithful warrior. Thy work shall be rewarded. The most able knights and squires to be found in the kingdom shall be at thy command."

"Thank you, Your Majesty. I shall begin at once to search out the best in the kingdom."

Holding up his trusted sabre, the king declared, "Thou fightest with sword, shield, and spear, but thy greatest weapons be truth and righteousness. When thou trainest the young men of the kingdom, thou art training the future fathers and husbands—the heads of marriages, the foundation of families, and the strength of the kingdom. Blessings, Sir Valiant. Continue, I charge thee, to fight the good fight. Do not give up when the way is hard. Persevere and never forget the One who is a rewarder of all who seek Him."

"May all the kingdom hear thy wisdom," Sir Valiant replied. "Thy command shall I do with all my strength."

A Purpose Worth Living For

As I walked down the path, I was especially conscious this day that I was alone. There was no male friend walking beside me. There was no male friend in my life at all. Nor had there ever been. This particular day it seemed hard to wait. I was feeling discouraged.

Had you been there, I would have quickly told you that I was not actually discouraged. After all, the Lord was doing wonderful things in my life. Our family was in the middle of a ministry trip, and I was excited to see the Lord working. I was confident that I was exactly where God wanted me to be.

As I was walking along and struggling with these thoughts rushing through my mind, I was also "lecturing" myself that I had every reason in the world to be rejoicing. Why was I discouraged? It was a beautiful day. Why wasn't I enjoying it? Why did I feel like crying?

I was asking the Lord for help and suddenly He gave me a new thought—or maybe I should say He reminded me of an old one. My ultimate goal in life is not to be happy. My goal is to glorify God. After all, I was created for *His* pleasure, not my own. I don't need to try to be happy, and in one sense it really doesn't even matter whether I feel happy or not. (Of course, God *does* desire for us to be happy, but our focus should not be on *trying* to be happy, but on doing God's will—which is what brings true happiness.) I decided, "My goal today is not to be happy. My goal is to make other people happy. I'm going to look for ways to encourage and serve others—and most of all, to praise and glorify the Lord." As I made this decision, the Lord reminded me that it is by giving to others that we ourselves are blessed. When we forget our own desires and concentrate on pouring out our lives in service for others, He then fills us with inexpressible joy. For you see, loving God and others is what makes us happy (Jn. 15:12). Loving ourselves simply makes us lonely.

Many women look back on their single years and say, "Oh, if only I had used them wisely. If only I had understood what a treasure my single years were and had not wasted them by just longing to be married."

I don't know about you, but if I get married someday, I want to be able to look back on my single years and see that I used them wisely, enjoyed each day, and made the most of every opportunity. My prayer is that I would be a trustworthy steward of the gift of singleness that God has given me.

One of the biggest dangers we can fall into is the one the princess was struggling with when she allowed the seed of Discontent in her heart: the danger of self-pity. The more she felt sorry for herself, the worse she felt, and the more she allowed self-pity to grow, the more she was consumed by her own problems and thus lost her focus on other people.

My friend Melissa recently sent me an e-mail. She explained to me how her father had made a decision that she didn't like, and she began to feel discontented with the father the Lord had given her. Melissa went on to say that because she didn't respond properly to this wrong thought about her dad, but allowed her angry feelings to continue, the discontentment only increased. Soon she felt discontent with both her parents, her brothers and sisters, the size of their home, and even her own personality. Without even realizing what she was doing, she began to blame God for all these areas that didn't meet her "approval." The enemy was using thoughts of discontentment to discourage her, hinder her relationship with the Lord, and cause her to make wrong decisions. One thing that she noticed at this time was that she was easily irritated. She said that instead of focusing on the good in other people, she was only noticing the bad. In addition, she found herself often fostering a negative attitude and criticizing others. Melissa told me that it wasn't until she had hurt several people in her family (including herself) by her critical spirit that she realized where she had gone wrong, repented of these wrong thoughts, and began giving thanks to God rather than complaining. Do you see the dangerous consequences of the seed of Discontent?

The king understood this danger and knew the best answer to give the princess. Her focus needed to shift from herself to others. When she concentrated on the work her heavenly Father had called her to do, her joy increased. Her needs were forgotten and others took precedence in her life.

If thou are not fighting the King's battles,
thou shalt never meet the King's daughter.

The Potential of Your Youth

If your single years are spent simply waiting around for Prince Charming, feeling sorry for yourself, and dreaming of being married, your life will be miserable. But if your days are spent serving the Lord, each day will only get *sweeter* as you abide in His presence, more *joyous* as you see His plans for you unfold, and more *fulfilling* as you learn that it is more blessed to give than to receive (Acts 20:35).

Many young ladies have shared with me the joy they have received from serving others. For example, a fifteen-year-old girl who decided to start a Bright Lights group to minister to younger girls in her area sent me the following e-mail:

"You know, I think making this decision to start a Bright Lights group has been one of the very best decisions I have made in my life. I feel so good. It's like I finally have found something that I can do for the Lord, and He wants me to do this. He is just filling me with joy. Like I told my mom yesterday, I have never felt like I had a purpose in life, something that I could do for the Lord, and now the Lord is just filling me with joy. It is *so* wonderful."

Few people realize how valuable these single years can be for the kingdom of God. Teenagers today seem to have the idea that the teen years are a time when it's okay to be irresponsible. Many parents seem to *expect* that these years will be full of problems, rebellion, and struggles. This mindset is completely opposite to what the Lord desires our teen years to be like. In I Timothy 4:12, we are told, *"Let no man despise thy youth, but be thou an example of the believers, in word, in conversation, in charity, in spirit, in faith, in purity."*

The years of your youth are some of the most valuable ones of your life. If you can catch a vision for how much potential these years have for the Lord, you will begin to feel that your life is a race—a race against time to accomplish as much as you possibly can for the kingdom of God. After all, when the years of your youth are gone, they have vanished forever. You'll never have a second chance to relive them. Remember also that your youth will determine your future. The decisions you make now will affect your entire life.

Not only are these years valuable, but they are also powerful. The world will often listen to young people more quickly than they will listen to adults. Mature and wise youths stand out in today's culture; they are noticed and their voice is heard. Few young people realize this potential power that they have. As a young and single person, devote yourself to the work of the Lord. You do not yet have the responsibilities of marriage; you have energy; you have time. Since these years have so much potential, one of the most important qualities for you to be developing as a single young lady is diligence! Learn to rise early, to establish good personal disciplines, and to use each minute wisely in order to do as much as you can to further Christ's kingdom! Do not waste this time of singleness! *"The unmarried woman careth for the things of the Lord, that she may be holy both in body and in spirit: but she that is married careth for the things of the world, how she may please her husband. And this I speak for your own profit; not that I may cast a snare upon you, but for that which is comely, and that ye may attend upon the Lord without distraction"* (I Cor. 7:34–35).

Right now I'm twenty-six years old; I've never dated or started any serious relationship with a young man. The years of singleness I've had so far have been exciting and amazing—I would never want to trade them. Of course, I want to get married, but I also know that singleness is a gift, that God's timing is perfect, and that it is for Him to decide if and when I am to marry. It never helps to be in a hurry. God is giving us opportunities right now that we will never have again.

What about those who never marry? This is a horrible thought for many young ladies. Yet if we have the right perspective, there is no need to fear a life of singleness. Rather, we can be excited to know that if it is God's plan for us to be single, He is calling us to some special ministry for the Lord. Therefore, in that sense, singleness is a gift that is very profitable and fulfilling. Remember also that many who are married are unhappily married. Marriage, in and of itself, is not what gives purpose and meaning in life, but rather fulfillment comes from walking with and serving the Lord.

RUN THE RACE WITH PERSEVERANCE

Our family was on a tight schedule, in the middle of a busy city, at a crowded time of day, and trying to get to a certain destination before it closed. As we were walking briskly and looking frequently at our watches, we suddenly encountered a problem.

"Oh, great," said Stephen. "There's a parade in our way. Now what?"

"There's no way to get across the street," I sighed. "I guess we're stuck."

"I suppose we'll have to turn around," Grace said disappointedly.

"We could just wait and watch the parade," Mom suggested.

"We'll never make it on time," Dad and Stephen said simultaneously.

We stood looking at each other for a minute and acting a little bewildered. Then Dad suddenly spoke up, "I think we can still get there on time. Let's see if we can catch up with the front of the parade and head them off. Hurry! Follow me!"

"I don't think this is a good idea," said Stephen, "Look at all these crowds of—"

But Dad was already out of sight. "Quick," Stephen said to the rest of us. "This way." And we were off. All five of us, carrying our various purses and bags, began to maneuver through the crowds. "Excuse me, excuse me, pardon me ... oh, excuse me, ma'am," Dad was saying, creating a path for the rest of us to follow. We had a hard time keeping up with him. Soon we were all out of breath, but Dad and Stephen were up in front going in and out of shops along the sidewalk, squeezing through tight places, and trying to find shortcuts. We were following behind, trying not to lose them.

I'm sure that the five of us were pretty conspicuous to the bystanders as we raced by. But we didn't have time to be embarrassed or concerned about what people thought of us. And we didn't stick around long enough to hear any of their remarks.

At last we reached the front of the parade. "Quick," said Dad, stepping over some yellow caution tape, "let's cross the street here." Exhausted and out of breath, we arrived at our destination—and even had a couple minutes to spare! I think it was more fun (and definitely more memorable) trying to *get* to our destination than it was after we arrived there.

Our family marathon reminded me of how often we are tempted

to give up on a plan as soon as we encounter an obstacle. It reminded me that surprising things can be achieved through absolute dedication and an unwavering focus on our final goal. Initiative. Determination. Creativity. Courage. Leadership. These are qualities God honors. He wants us to have a "race" mentality in this life, running with perseverance, doing as much as we can for His glory, making the most of every opportunity, knowing that time is short (Heb. 12:1–2, Eph. 5:16, Acts 20:24).

Many people (even Christians) reach the end of life and feel that they have wasted many years—or accomplished nothing at all. This is often because they did not have vision for what the Lord could do through their lives. They lost sight of their ultimate purpose for being on this earth, and as a result, they were lax in their use of time, easily distracted by the things of the world, slow to take initiative, and inattentive to the needs around them.

If we don't have a plan, we won't go anywhere. If we give up when the way gets hard, our strength is small (Prov. 24:10). If we quit as soon as we hit a roadblock, we definitely are not going to make it very far. If we turn around when things look hopeless, we've lost sight of our all-powerful God. If we admit defeat when we're tired, we've forgotten that we're in the middle of a war. Every day contains small, yet significant, battles for the Lord. Fix your eyes on the finish line, persevere, give your all to the Master, and know that He who has called you will be faithful to do the work (I Thess. 5:24). When we stand before the Lord one day, we will not regret any sacrifice we have made for Him. We will only wish we had given Him more.

Your Life Purpose

I don't know what your home is like, but at our house Sunday mornings can be kind of hectic and unorganized. Since certain members of our family like to be early, and certain other ones seem to have a different definition of the word, we finally have come up with a workable plan. We take two cars to church. One car leaves on time with anyone who is in it. And the other one leaves … well, whenever it leaves. One particular Sunday morning, as we were all scurrying around trying to get ready for church, looking for something quick for breakfast, and waiting to jump into the bathroom the second it was available, we heard my dad open the side door and call out, "Hey! What's this?"

"What's what?" we asked.

"Someone left two white envelopes on our porch last night."

The regular business-sized envelopes we found on the step were damp from dew and obviously had been on the step all night. Stephen's name was written on one envelope. After bomb and anthrax testing (just kidding), we brought them in and carefully opened them. One contained a large object like a cell phone and the other some electronic cables. We were all puzzled for a minute as we examined the small device.

"What is it?" Mom asked. "Is it a video game?"

"Maybe a new kind of cell phone or a walkie talkie," I suggested.

"Hey! I know!" said Stephen. "It's a GPS module."

(We had never seen one before, but we knew what they were.) We wondered who might have given it to us. Our family travels frequently, so a GPS module is a very helpful tool to have on hand. By connecting to satellites in orbit, a GPS module is able to tell you exactly where you are. If you plug it into your laptop and use a map program, you can track your position and find exact directions to your destination. We never found out who left the envelope outside our door, but we were very grateful for the surprise gift!

If you are lost, the first thing you need to find out is where you are! Directions are not any help unless you know not only where you want to end up, but also where you are now. Most young people need a spiritual GPS module to give them some guidance. They have no purpose in life. They do not know what they want to do with their future, how to get there, where they are now, or why they are here. Without purpose in life we wander aimlessly, either allowing slothfulness to take control or finding ourselves "busy" but accomplishing very little.

Take inventory and ask yourself where you are right now. Why does God have you here? What is His purpose for you today? What is His calling for your life? And how are you going to get to your next destination?

Maybe you're all confused about your life and have no idea what the Lord's plan is for you. Maybe you feel like I did one night when I was thirteen. Returning from a Christian conference, I climbed into bed, turned off the lights, and prayed, "Lord, what do you want me to do? Lord, I want to serve You. I *really* want to serve You. But how? What am I supposed to be doing? Lord, please use me somehow for Your glory." I had no idea what God had in store for my life. All I remember is that I wanted to somehow, in some way, serve the Lord.

But here is the important point: I didn't know what the Lord had in store for my life, but I **did** know that there were some areas in my life in which I needed to be obedient. First, there were some people I had wronged, and I knew the Lord wanted me to go and ask their forgiveness. Then there were some spiritual disciplines (such as Bible reading, Scripture memorization, prayer, etc.) that I knew I needed to more diligently apply in my life. As I began to obey the Lord in these "small" areas, He began to open more and more ministry doors for me.

It will be the same for you. The Lord usually doesn't show us the whole picture of our life right away, but He is always faithful to show us the next step. Each act of obedience opens new doors of ministry and reveals the next step God wants us to take. This is walking by faith—trusting the Lord with all our heart, acknowledging Him, and knowing that He will direct our paths. It requires obedience on our part. But we must not think that we can skip any of the steps along the way. Obey now and you will reap the rewards later.

As a young lady, you probably believe that God is calling you to be a wife and mother. This is a very noble calling. In fact, there is no assignment more important than raising a new generation to serve the Lord. Yet, marriage cannot be your ultimate goal in life. You must have a life purpose bigger than marriage. If you don't, you won't be fully prepared for marriage.

Of course, I don't mean just any "life purpose." I am definitely not referring to seeking after a career. Our culture, driven by the modern feminist movement, is pressuring us as girls to be successful in the world's eyes, get graduate degrees, be independent, move up in the business world, have small families, and do men's work. This standard of success that the world pushes does not even compare to the calling

God has for our lives as wives and mothers. God made us to be helpers to our husbands and to bear and train little ones for the kingdom of God. This is far more important and fulfilling than any career could ever be.

So what do I mean by "a life purpose bigger than marriage"? I mean that our life purpose must be to serve the Lord, to give our entire lives to Him, and to bear much eternal fruit in order to bring God glory (Jn. 15:8). Unless we are focused on this "great work" (Neh. 6:3) for God, we will never be fulfilled in either singleness or marriage.

There are many people God brings into our paths each day who desperately need the gospel, teaching, and encouragement. Purpose to have a ministry mindset everywhere you go.

A BROKEN ELEVATOR

"We actually have a free afternoon," Dad said, "and this is our last day in Florida before leaving for home. We have been wanting to visit our friend, Clorinda. Let's go now." (Clorinda is an eighty-some-year-old lady who has been friends with our family for many years.)

"We should take the harps with us and play for her," Dad suggested as he, Grace, and I were climbing into the van.

"Okay," we said. We were not at all surprised by my dad's idea. He believes in—as he would say—"being prepared." If at all possible, he takes ministry tools everywhere we go.

"And since we have the space, we may as well take the chalk easel too," Dad added.

"Why not?" I said with a smile.

An hour or so later, we arrived at Clorinda's assisted-living complex, took the elevator up to the third floor, and took a seat in her small living room.

"I've been praying for all my friends here in this complex," she told us. "Most of them know very little about the Bible. When I heard that your family was coming to Florida, I asked the staff if we could arrange a harp program or chalk talk in our meeting room downstairs. But unfortunately, they said they had a policy against outside religious groups. I asked several times—but I always got a firm 'no.' "

"Well, how about if we just bring our harps up to your room

and play for you?" we suggested. "You could invite some of your friends over to listen. We'll be able to share a Christian testimony by introducing a few of our songs and telling some things about our ministry."

Very much enthused by this idea, Clorinda picked up the phone right away to invite a friend over. Then Dad, Grace, and Clorinda went downstairs to get the harps. But when they pushed the down button for the elevator, nothing happened. They waited several minutes, but the elevator never arrived. "I guess we'll have to take the stairs," Clorinda concluded. When they arrived at ground level, they noticed the commotion in the lobby. "The elevator is broken!" was the big news.

"But how are we going to bring the harps up to Clorinda's room without an elevator?" Grace asked. That is when they realized that God was arranging something.

Dad found one of the staff and asked, "Sir, we brought our harps to play for our friend Clorinda, but your elevator doesn't seem to be working. We can't take the harps up the stairs, so do you think we could just play for her right here in the lobby?"

"Well, since the elevator isn't working, uh, sure—go right ahead," he answered.

"Or maybe it would be better if we set it up in the meeting room," Dad suggested. "That way if some other people would like to hear the music, there would be room for them to sit down and listen."

"No problem," the staff replied. "There's nothing planned for the meeting room today."

Dad moved in the harps, Grace and I started tuning, and Clorinda began making calls! Soon a group of about thirty people had made their way into the meeting room, and Grace and I started playing. Since everyone was listening quietly, it was a perfect opportunity to introduce each song and share about the Lord.

When Dad realized what a large group of people had assembled, he found a staff member, and wording his request carefully, explained, "You know, sir, often when the girls play their harps they also do a chalk presentation. Grace accompanies on the harp as Sarah draws a picture on a large easel and tells some stories about the Bible. We happen to have our easel right out in the van. I could set it up in a few minutes. I think a lot of the people here would enjoy it."

"Oh, really? That'd be great!" the man answered—much to Dad's amazement.

Out of the corner of my eye, I noticed Dad bringing in the easel. He set it up as we were playing, and then I started drawing. I drew a picture of a mountain scene with a waterfall, illustrating a message on the faithfulness and power of God. In the presentation, we told a number of stories, clearly explained the gospel, and Grace shared her salvation testimony.

Just then the head director stepped into the back of the room to observe what was happening. Dad nervously walked over to him and started to explain a little about what we were doing. But there was no need to fear.

"If I'd known you were coming," the director said, "we could have advertised this! Let us know if you're ever in the area again. We'd love to have you back." He then began taking pictures.

Dad ended our presentation in prayer—but no one wanted us to leave. We were amazed at how well they responded. And then, as soon as the presentation was over, guess what happened? The elevator started working!

Clorinda, who is zealous for the Lord and has a fiery personality, was so excited that she couldn't stop talking about how God broke the elevator! In fact, she was so energized that she was walking (almost jumping) around—without her cane. She didn't even notice that she had left it behind! As we were loading up the van in the parking lot, Clorinda stamped her foot on the ground with enthusiasm and proclaimed, "Today was a victory for the Lord Jesus Christ. Satan tried to stop us, but Jesus stomped upon his head."

"Thank you for coming," one staff member told us, almost teary-eyed. "The elevator never breaks like this. I know that it broke just at the right time so that you could play your harps for us. The only problem," he continued, "is that I already called the repair man to fix the elevator—and he's on his way. He's traveling over an hour to get here. I don't know what I'm going to tell him. I guess I'll just have to explain that God broke the elevator and then fixed it again."

As we pulled out of the parking lot, we all marveled at what God had done. "I can tell that Clorinda has been praying for this place," I said. "Think of all the details the Lord worked out for us today. We *just happened* to have the afternoon free. I *just happened* to have a sheet of chalk paper all prepared. (Chalk drawing takes some advance preparation—sanding and pre-chalking.) The meeting room *just happened* to be available. And the elevator *just happened* to break at the exact moment that we needed to move the harps upstairs."

Later we were told that the repair man couldn't find anything wrong with the elevator. Hmmm ... I wonder why?

The Lord has given each of us different skills, talents, interests, and tools. Develop the ones God has given you, and look for ways to use them to advance Christ's kingdom. Your tools don't need to be things like harps or easels. In fact, often the Lord chooses to use the very smallest things—a tract, a smile, a kind word, a Bible verse, or a personal testimony. If you do the necessary preparation, such as developing talents and skills God can use, He will open up doors (or break elevators) for you to use them. My parents have always encouraged me and my siblings to see the needs of the people around us and to take initiative to meet those needs. They often remind us to turn everyday situations into opportunities to minister to others. Sometimes it just takes a little creativity!

In conclusion to this chapter, here are five main points to remember:

- Your youth can be a very productive time.
  When Jesus was twelve, He was already focused on being about His heavenly Father's business (Lk. 2:49).
- Be successful in singleness.
  If you are not successful in singleness, how can you ever expect to be successful in the new trials and challenges that marriage will bring? (Mt. 25:23)
- Ministry will prepare you for marriage.
  In more ways than you can imagine, serving the Lord now will prepare and equip you to one day be a godly wife and mother.
- Experience in ministry will give you greater discernment.

Ministering to others gives you a new ability to discern spiritual needs and develops the wisdom required to understand and evaluate a potential marriage partner.

- Put God's work first and He will take care of everything else.
  "But seek ye first the kingdom of God, and His righteousness; and all these things shall be added unto you" (Mt. 6:33).

*Only he who traineth for battle
winneth the hand of the princess.*

SUGGESTED MEMORY VERSE:

"But seek ye first the kingdom of God, and His righteousness; and all these things shall be added unto you" (Matthew 6:33).

SUGGESTED ASSIGNMENT:

God gives each Christian messages to share. Our primary message is the gospel, but there are other specific matters God will impress upon you that He wants you to share with others. Corrie ten Boom spoke about forgiveness. Hudson Taylor spoke about missions. Today there are many individuals God has raised up who are faithfully sharing particular messages the Lord has given them—messages including topics such as creation science, marriage, sharing your faith, Biblical worldview, principles of finances, the reliability of Scripture, and the list goes on.

Ask the Lord what messages He has given you to share with others. What verses has He used in your life? What major lessons has He taught you? What needs has He burdened you with? Each of these can become life messages.

Choose one topic, perhaps the testimony of what brought you to salvation, and begin to prepare it. Be ready to share it with people God brings into your path. Maybe it is something you could share at a Sunday school class or youth group, or in a tract, letter, or family newsletter. God will give you opportunities. But your job is to prepare.

CHAPTER NINE

Dreams Must Die

"For whosoever will save his life shall lose it;
and whosoever will lose his life for My sake shall find it."
Matthew 16:25

There alone on the balcony, the princess spent several hours in thought and in prayer. She loved the peaceful feeling of the west balcony covered with vines, sweet peas, and ivy. It seemed like her own private place, outdoors—yet nearly indoors. She had so many memories of special times of prayer she had enjoyed there alone, admiring the view of the mountains and talking with the One who had created them.

As she listened to the birds and felt the gentle breeze, she was vividly reminded of what she already knew—that her life was not her own, for she had been bought with a price. In that still and quiet moment, she made an important decision in her heart. She determined *that regardless of the cost, she must take the higher road. With renewed zeal, she once again dedicated her life, her time, and her future to her heavenly Father and to whatever work He saw fit to give her.*

Joyfully, she returned to the palace, anxious to tell her father of her decision not only to remain home from the Merchants' Fest, but more importantly, to serve her Master with a greater fervor than ever before.

The princess had yet to learn that when one struggle is overcome, the next one is usually just around the corner. For, as she hurried through the courtyard, instead of finding her father, she encountered the last person she ever would have expected.

It was, as you may have guessed, Sir Valiant. He had finished a lengthy conference with her father and was just mounting his horse to depart from the castle, dedicated in his service for the king.

The princess stopped suddenly. Then she quickly smiled and cheerfully exclaimed, "Oh, hello!" Though her voice was calm, her heart was trembling, and dozens of questions raced through her mind. What shall I say? Shall I introduce myself? Why is he here? Does he know who I am?

Her anxiousness was forgotten, however, when Valiant dismounted his horse, returned her greeting, and said, "Oh, and you must be the king's daughter? I have heard so much about you. Many in the village speak of thy virtue and kindness."

The princess laughed and replied, "Oh, well, I have heard about you as well. My father says thou art among his most trustworthy knights. He deeply values thy loyal service."

The princess thought that Sir Valiant looked more handsome and radiant than ever as he stood there in the bright sunlight. In reality, if she could have seen herself, she would have been equally surprised to see the brightness of her own face. It is perhaps a good thing that the princess did not realize that her beauty was only becoming more and more radiant with time.

The two of them did not talk long, but as the princess waved good-bye and watched him ride away, she felt as if her heart would burst. She had never felt that way before. She turned away and floated—well, almost—into the palace to see the king.

In her excitement, the princess had forgotten the news she had planned to tell her father about her commitment to dedicate her life anew to her heavenly King. A host of new thoughts were now rushing through her mind. She nearly ran over her father as she entered the palace and found him speaking with her mother.

The king smiled and seemed to already guess what the princess was thinking. She asked him all about Sir Valiant—why he had come, when he would be back, how long he had been serving in the king's army, and where he was from. She wanted to ask many more questions—whether the king would like him for a son-in-law, whether they had spoken of her, and whether he was courting anyone else—but she thought it better to say nothing.

The princess was excited all week, wondering when Sir Valiant might return and if she might be able to get to know him better. But soon the reality of daily life began to set in, and she started to wonder why she had been so quick to imagine that he was the one for her. Surely she had been foolish to entertain such thoughts.

Diligently, the princess gave herself to eternal things—sewing clothes for the poor, spending time with orphans, representing her father at important gatherings, and providing much hospitality for guests and ambassadors visiting the castle. But once again the princess found herself growing tired of waiting. The months seemed to drag by slowly, and she sometimes found herself discouraged. "What am I even waiting for?" she wondered. "Is it possible, as the alligator has so often said, that I am waiting for a dream that will never come true?"

After finishing dinner one cloudy evening, the princess decided to take a walk along the path that went past the courtyard, through the vineyard, and along the edge of the forest outside the castle. So many questions troubled her. So many fears found their way into her thoughts. She remembered the afternoon out on the balcony only six months earlier. She had been so excited about living each day to the fullest, so determined to be content, no matter what. Now it felt as if she had been waiting forever.

But Sir Valiant was so handsome and perfect. How could she help but notice him? All her dreams rushed back fresh and new—

love letters, romantic walks by starlight, a diamond ring, a glorious wedding, staring into her prince's eyes, being held tightly in his arms, being a mother, and oh, her longings were almost too overwhelming for her to bear.

Hearing soft footsteps, she turned around and saw her mother walking behind her. The princess waited but said nothing, telling herself that she was determined not to start crying.

Her mother seemed to already know how she was feeling, as mothers usually do, and gently asked if everything was all right.

The princess was silent for a few moments and then began to speak slowly. "Years ago I decided that I had a purpose in life much bigger than marriage and that I would gladly stay single if my heavenly Father asked this of me. Time after time, I have prayed for His will to be done and purposed to be content. And just when I thought I had finally understood contentment, just when I thought I had finally learned how to patiently wait, Sir Valiant came to visit, and ... and ... and made everything harder. I just don't understand why I can't learn to trust and am so easily distracted. And why—" she concluded with a sigh, "why does this have to be so difficult?"

"Struggles are a necessary part of life," her mother said. "They strengthen us and prepare us for the new trials that lie ahead. When one struggle is overcome, another is often around the next bend."

"I suppose. But Mother, I feel like I'm failing in each struggle, not overcoming them."

"Thou art growing. Thou art learning. These are the very things the struggle is designed to accomplish in thy life. Do not forget, dear daughter, that except a corn of wheat fall into the ground and die, it abideth alone: but if it die, it bringeth forth much fruit."

"Bear fruit—that is exactly what I want to do," the princess said quietly, as if deep in thought.

"Then your dream must die."

"But my dream is a good dream, not a bad dream. It is the dream God has given me. It is nothing wicked I desire, but only what is natural, wholesome, and beautiful. Why must it die?"

Her mother stepped off the path, knelt down, picked up an acorn, and explained, "Observe this acorn, perfectly designed for what

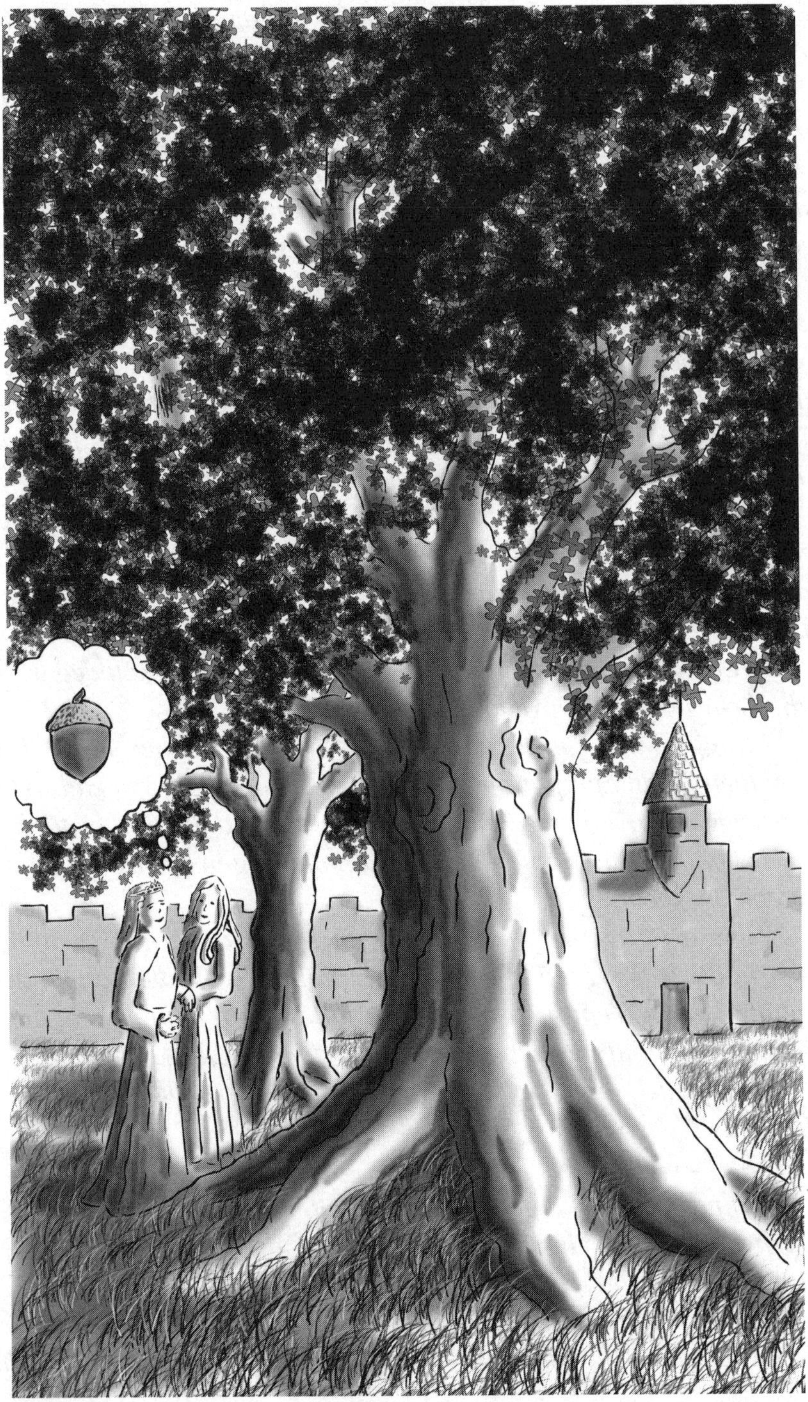

it is intended to do—die. The acorn does not know why; the acorn does not understand what is ahead, but only if it is buried in the cold and dark earth—forgotten and left alone—does it fulfill its purpose and become what it was created to be. Would the acorn ever have imagined that it would become the beautiful oak tree you see before you? Not in its wildest dreams. When you admire the oak tree, do you mourn the loss of the acorn? Of course not. By losing its life, the acorn became something so much greater, so much more beautiful, so much more valuable. The death is forgotten. The fruit is remembered. Nevertheless, death was required."

Intense Desires

I was sitting in the living room when my fourteen-year-old brother Stephen walked in and, out of the blue, brought up one of his favorite discussion topics—new computer equipment.

"You know, Sarah," he commented, "for *me*, getting a laptop would sort of be like *you* getting married!"

A little surprised by his analogy, I looked up from whatever it was that I was doing and said, "Uh, I wouldn't quite make that comparison, but what makes you say that?"

"Well," Stephen continued, "getting a laptop is something I've always looked forward to, and I won't be able to believe it if it actually happens."

"Hmmm … but, Stephen, what about you getting married?" I asked.

"Sarah, that would be like you getting a laptop," he responded. Stephen walked out of the room, and I sat there smiling.

Even though I'm not sure I agree with Stephen's analogy, he was right about one thing. The Lord has given young ladies the desire to be married. This is a good desire—a God-given desire. Most of us *will* get married some day, and we can be grateful that the Lord has given us a longing for the very thing He has called us to do.

All the same, marriage is not our ultimate goal. A husband is not what will make us happy, and marriage is not what will bring true fulfillment in life.

Even girls who are very young are often led to believe that a boyfriend is what will make them happy. One hot summer day I was having a conversation with a friend in my neighborhood. I was eleven years old and she was nine. The Lord had been working in my life that summer, and I wanted to tell my friend about Jesus.

"Let's go for a walk, Hannah," I suggested.

As I was walking beside her, squinting in the bright sunlight, and trying to keep the conversation going, I was silently asking myself, "What can I say? I want to witness, but how?"

Finally, I thought of a question to ask her. "What do you want more than anything else in the world, Hannah?" I said.

She paused a moment, and then confidently answered, "A boyfriend!"

This sort of caught me by surprise. After all, I was only eleven and she was only nine! She thought a boyfriend would bring happiness and meaning to her life. Even though she was young, she knew her life was missing something, and she was looking for fulfillment. She needed to know that Jesus Christ was the only One who could fill that void in her heart.

In the same way, when we have unfulfilled longings in our lives, we often look in the wrong places for help. We think that happiness will be found when all our "wants" have been obtained. Thus, we spend our lives attempting to have our desires met, our dreams fulfilled, and our wishes come to pass.

But instead of seeking after these "wants," the Lord gives us some radically different guidance. As usual, God's thinking and the world's thinking are exactly opposite. The world says, "Follow your dreams. Seek whatever will make you happy." God says, "Surrender everything and count it gain" (Lk. 14:33, 18:29–30). The world says, "You deserve to get what you want." God says, "Whoever loses his life, finds it" (Matt. 16:25).

As single young ladies, it's important to realize that a husband will not make us happy. Nor is marriage a right that God is "supposed" to give us. Marriage is a gift.

Moreover, our purpose in getting married must not be to *get*, but rather to *give*. While we are on this earth, we will always experience unfulfilled longings (Rom. 8:23). God intends for these desires to draw us to Himself. The Lord knows that He is the only One who can satisfy our hearts. He completes us. He wants us to know and experience the reality that He is enough. He desires that we learn unconditional surrender.

The Greatest Exchange

Riding home in our minivan, I could hardly stop talking about my ideas. I leaned forward in the back seat and tried to explain all my new thoughts to Mom and Dad, talking loudly in order to be heard over the sound of our noisy van and my energetic siblings. Our family was on the way home from a conference where I had been asked to share about the Bright Lights ministry. I had been overwhelmed by the response of many young ladies who had talked with me afterwards and was very surprised to hear that so many other girls were interested in beginning a Bright Lights group in their area. I was twenty-one years old at the time. Up to this point, there were no other Bright Lights groups except for the three that I was leading. Suddenly, I realized that the Lord was opening new doors and expanding this ministry to girls. Not only was God generating interest in others, He was giving me an excitement and vision for what was ahead.

I was flooded with ideas. First of all, there was a need for discipleship materials for mothers and daughters. There was also a need for resources for leaders and training conferences for older girls. In addition, I could see mother/daughter conferences as a way to reach young ladies on a wider scale. And, well, there seemed to be no end to the possibilities that the Lord might have in store. I was so excited about what God was doing, I could hardly think about anything else!

As the weeks went by, I began to realize that some of my ideas were rather unrealistic and that many obstacles had to be overcome. I began to wonder whether all these ideas were really from the Lord or just my own dreams. I began to search my heart and evaluate whether my motive was truly to reach young ladies or to gain something for myself. I desperately wanted to *want* only what the Lord wanted, but I was confused. My dreams seemed to be from the Lord—yet I also knew how easily prideful and selfish motives could creep in.

I distinctly remember one day just a few weeks later when I got on my knees and made a list of all my ideas and dreams for Bright Lights—every little desire and every big dream. I put them all on my list. Then, one by one, I surrendered them to the Lord, asking that He would purify my heart and use me to accomplish *His* purposes, not my own. Finally, I ripped up the paper and asked the Lord to exchange my dreams with His will—whatever it might be. I still had a strong desire to minister to young ladies, and I still felt that the Lord was leading me to pursue the vision He had given, but I also knew that if the Lord's plans were different than mine, He could be trusted. Even if none of my ideas came to pass, I was resolved to put my whole heart into His assignments and follow His leading.

Several years later it suddenly dawned on me that every single one of those dreams had come to pass. And even more exciting to me was the fact that dozens of other ministry opportunities that had never even crossed my mind had also been part of the Lord's bigger plan. Waiting was involved, and God's timing was definitely different than mine. In fact, some things that I hoped would happen immediately took nearly five years, but in hindsight it is clear that God sees the whole picture and writes the last chapter.

Surrender is a daily part of the Christian life. The Lord is jealous for us with a godly jealousy and desires to have first place in every area of our hearts (Ex. 34:14). He will quickly ask us to surrender any possession, person, interest, career, activity, or dream that begins to take priority. Sometimes He gives our dreams back; sometimes He doesn't. It is His intense love, His desire for our ultimate happiness, and His understanding of what will bring forth the most fruit, that necessitates this pruning—which may appear to us as unmerciful, unfair, and painful.

There are many things besides my goals for Bright Lights that the Lord has asked me to surrender. I have found this same exercise of writing a list of dreams and ripping it up helpful in the area of marriage. One day several years ago, I wrote out every dream I could think of (from the smallest little desires, such as a romantic evening, to the biggest desires, such as being a mother and raising children), and after specifically surrendering each "dream" to the Lord, I ripped up the list, telling the Lord that I wanted to exchange my dreams with His will—no matter what this might entail. His will is infinitely better than my dream. It might not be what I would choose. It might not include marriage, but it is better. In fact, it is *so much better* that it is not even worthy to be compared with my finite viewpoint (II Cor. 4:17–18).

In Philippians 3:8, Paul says, *"Yea doubtless, and I count all things but loss for the excellency of the knowledge of Christ Jesus my Lord: for whom I have suffered the loss of all things, and do count them but dung, that I may win Christ."*

Shattered Dreams

A confused twenty-one-year-old girl thought frequently about the man she loved. But did he love her? They had dated for three years. He had asked her to marry him. She had joyfully agreed. The wedding date was set—and then—her dreams were shattered. He had changed his mind. Or at least he had changed his mind for the time being. He said he still loved her, but he wasn't ready to get married. He postponed the wedding. Worst of all, he postponed it indefinitely! She had no idea when he would actually decide—if ever! She might be waiting for the rest of her life.

With embarrassment, this young woman called off her wedding plans. Then she wondered what she should do next. She couldn't just sit around waiting for him to decide, so she took a job teaching at a Christian school. She left him in Indiana, took off her engagement ring, and moved to Florida. As the months went by, the waiting got harder. She was still in love, but was her love returned? She wasn't sure.

As she continued to struggle, she finally realized that she couldn't go through the rest of her life like this—just waiting, wondering, and worrying. One evening she got down on her knees and began to pray. With tears she surrendered her dreams, her future, and this young man to the Lord. She purposed to trust the Lord's plan no matter what and to say, "Not my will, but Thine be done."

She stood up and just a few minutes later the phone rang. It was him!!! He had decided to get married at last. The plans were made. The wedding day arrived. They said, "I do." Eventually they had a baby—ME! It wasn't until my mother surrendered to the Lord her desire to marry that He answered her prayers and gave her the godly husband she had longed for.

It is not only our sin and wrong desires that God asks us to give up. He asks for everything. Every part of our heart. Every area of our life. Since He wants to have first place, the Lord will ask us to surrender anything that hinders our relationship with Him. It is not just the big areas He requests, but also the very smallest. A life of surrender is the sweetest one possible, while a life of stubbornness and unwillingness to yield is the most miserable. Yet, so many times we are slow to submit and to enter into the freedom and rest God wants to give.

When the sacrifice seems hard, pause and remember the One to whom you are surrendering. Don't dwell on your personal sacrifice, but rather consider the perfect faithfulness, loving-kindness, power, and beauty of the One who alone can satisfy us completely. Consider what He has given for us. Consider how much He deserves. When our mind is stayed upon Him, surrender becomes an act of pure joy. *"Again, the kingdom of heaven is like unto treasure hid in a field; the which when a man hath found, he hideth, and for **joy** thereof goeth and selleth all that he hath, and buyeth that field"* (Mt. 13:44, emphasis added).

In an e-mail I received recently, my friend shared with me the freedom that comes from simply surrendering to the Lord:

"I am so excited to see how God is blessing me as I've been surrendering to Him and letting Him be in control of things. I don't know, maybe it is that for so long I've just been trying to handle things on my own. Now I can see that even when I thought I was surrendering, I'd been trying to run the show. I have so much more joy and freedom now than I have had for a long time. And I haven't really made any huge sacrifices or anything; it's just that the little areas of life that I was trying to handle on my own, I am now learning to simply leave in His hands. You know, Sarah, I find that in the 'big' struggles, I tend to count on the Lord more because I know that I'm not able to do it on my own, but in the small things that I think I should be 'able' to handle, I forget to keep counting on Him. But I need Him just as much in the small stuff—especially if I want to be living a life that is totally glorifying to Him."

WHEN DYING IS TRUE LIVING

If you were asked to die for your faith, would you be willing to lay down your life? I assume that most of us would say we'd be willing to die for Christ. Yet I fear that we are not so willing to *live* for Christ. If we died today, we'd never have the opportunity to get married, raise a family, or see any of our other earthly dreams come to pass. We would understand this to be part of the sacrifice. We would have given our lives. That would mean everything.

Yet, are we willing to live our lives on earth and still sacrifice these same dreams and desires? Are we willing to joyfully stay single if that is what God asks us to do? To die to self? To count everything a loss in order to gain Christ?

Oftentimes we are quick to say we'll surrender in the "big" things: "Lord, I'll go anywhere for You—even to the jungles of Africa." But when it comes to the little, daily things, such as surrendering our friendships, forgiving a neighbor, or yielding what we want to do in order to serve others, we're not so ready to submit.

If the Lord asks us to sacrifice our best years to Him, if He asks us to wait when it seems that every other girl at church has a boyfriend, if He asks us to never be married ... are we willing? Any sacrifice we make for the Lord is not a loss, but a gain. We have been called to die that we might truly live, to lose our life that we might win it, to decrease that He might increase, and to surrender that we might gain the ultimate victory. After all, we are not our own. We have been bought with a price.

"Shall the thing formed say to him that formed it, Why hast thou made me thus? Hath not the potter power over the clay ... ?" (Rom. 9:20–21).

"Verily, verily, I say unto you, Except a corn of wheat fall into the ground and die, it abideth alone: but if it die, it bringeth forth much fruit" (Jn. 12:24).

SUGGESTED MEMORY VERSE:

"For whosoever will save his life shall lose it: and whosoever will lose his life for My sake shall find it" (Matthew 16:25).

SUGGESTED ASSIGNMENT:

Have some time alone with the Lord to specifically discuss with Him your dreams. Ask Him to purify your heart and direct your steps. Surrender any areas that you have been holding back for yourself. Acknowledge that you desire to do His will, rather than your own. As you surrender particular dreams, habits, activities, friendships, possessions, and plans, I'd encourage you to get out a journal and express your thoughts on paper. Write a letter to the Lord explaining your decision, yielding your will, and expressing your desire to be in complete submission to Him. Be specific in your letter as you discuss each area of struggle and lay it down at His feet. When you are tempted to "take back" areas you have previously surrendered, you can look back through your journal and be reminded of your decision and of how the Lord has worked in your heart.

CHAPTER TEN

Reserved for One

"For this is the will of God, even your sanctification, that ye should abstain from fornication: that every one of you should know how to possess his vessel in sanctification and honor."
I Thessalonians 4:3–4

"Well, well, here is the pitiful little princess coming back from the village," the alligator's cocky voice rang out as he sunned himself on the shore.

"Pitiful? Is that what thou thinkest of me?" asked the princess as Victory came to a stop. "I may be an acorn who needs to learn to die, and a rose who must stay closed until the proper time, but you do not need to feel sorry for me. If I could plan my own life, I would choose it to be no other way."

"You will continue, then, to tolerate your predicament of peril and distress?" questioned the alligator.

"What do you mean by peril and distress?" she asked.

"The current state of all unwed daughters, of course," the alligator replied with a smirk.

The princess neither answered nor smiled, so the alligator continued: "When your nonexistent hero does show up, he will think that because you have never been kissed, never been loved, never been swept off your feet, that apparently you are not worth the effort. No one has sought after you before—so why should he? Thou wilt be looked upon as a second-class, unwanted maiden."

"As far as I am concerned, any fellow who thinks that way may just as well go after some other maiden who is more lovable, more popular, more easily caught—and who has already given her heart to a dozen other Prince Charmings," she said, stroking Victory's mane.

"Listen to me for once," said the alligator in a more serious tone. "You say you will be pure—and perhaps you will be, living in this sheltered little prison. But, I tell you, your dreams will be shattered when you learn that your magnificent knight hath not done the same. Do you not see? You live in a changing world; there is not even one man alive who has saved himself for you. Search the whole world and I guarantee it, you will not find a single one."

"Even if you prove to be right, even if no true gentlemen yet exist, I still choose the way of purity. It is not an earthly knight for whom I ultimately save myself, but a heavenly One."

"Fine with me. Why should I care?" retorted the alligator. "I am going swimming."

The princess continued on her way inside, sat down on the velvet cushion in her favorite window seat, and opened her Bible. The rays of the late morning sun cast bright beams across its pages. She opened to the book of Psalms and tried to read, but soon she found herself daydreaming. Will my Prince Charming ever come? What if the alligator is right? What if no godly men exist? Unable to concentrate and feeling a little heavy hearted, she closed the Bible and went about her normal activities.

But as she was lying in bed that evening, she found herself wide awake. Although she knew the alligator was a liar, she could not seem to forget his words, and fearful thoughts about her future flooded her

mind. Sighing deeply and wiping a tear from her eye, she decided to talk with her parents. Sometimes she felt uncomfortable discussing her struggles with them, but she always felt better afterwards.

The princess slipped out of bed, wrapped her warm lavender robe around her, and stepped into her fur slippers. Then she lit her oil lamp and walked down the marble staircase. All was silent except for the trickling fountain in the Great Room. The guard smiled at her as she proceeded through the tall double doors into her parents' quarters. The king and queen were still awake talking, as she expected.

"Is everything well with you, dear one?" her mother asked. "You seemed quiet during dinner this evening."

The king came and sat beside her on the edge of the bed as the princess began to tell her parents of her most recent chat with the alligator.

"You will hear those same lies from many voices and in many forms," her father warned her. "But you must not listen to them for a minute. That which they speak is entirely contrary to the truth. Just when you are convinced that you must be the only devoted one alive, you find that the King of Kings has reserved for Himself seven thousand others—as He did long ago" (I Kgs. 19:14–18).

"Well, they must be hiding as they were then, because I surely have not met very many!" exclaimed the princess.

"Do not be discouraged by all the imperfect young men, dear," her mother comforted her. "After all, it only takes one to get married."

"But is it true what the alligator says, that men will look upon those who are pure as unwanted and thus less valuable?" the princess asked.

"Less valuable? Why, even common sense tells you that what you have waited for the longest you value the most," said the king. "A true gentleman wants to win your heart. He does not want you to come running up to him and pour it out freely. He wants to earn your respect and admiration, but you must give him the chance to try."

"Yes," continued the queen. "It is not such a changing world as the alligator wants you to believe. Wickedness has thrived since the Garden of Eden. The righteous have had to stand alone since the beginning of history. Young ladies have been trying to chase after

boys since the time of Genesis. By their anxiousness, they drive away the very men they would most like to catch. But the ones who are patient—who are willing to be sought after, who are willing to be a rosebud closed until the proper time—they are the most appealing, the most beautiful, the most treasured."

"And it is the same way for the men," her father added. "We must show patience as well. Think of how utterly foolish it would be if one went through the whole garden opening the flowers one by one, trying to enjoy the fragrance of all of them, and pulling apart each bud. Would they not be ruined?"

"God created mystery," explained her mother, as she gently pushed back the hair that was falling in the princess's face. "Things must be discovered. The most valuable treasures come through waiting. The mystery is part of the excitement. Many young ladies are far too ready to open their hearts before the time is right."

"Wait for the one who will fully appreciate the gift you have saved for him," the king advised.

"Guard your heart until you find the one to whom it may be wholly entrusted," the queen added. "Allow your hero the privilege of winning thy hand. In the end, he will value you more."

"And remember," said her father, placing his arm around her shoulders, "that you are set apart, first and foremost, for your heavenly Father—who loves and treasures you more than any knight ever could. Continue to delight thyself in His love."

A Purity So Bright the World Marvels

"Sarah," my mom said to me one afternoon when I was little, "you know Mr. and Mrs. Alden at our church? Well, did you know that their very first kiss was at their wedding? Just think how special it would be if you saved your first kiss for your wedding! I wish Daddy and I had done that."

I wasn't very old at the time, but I still remember the impact of her words. Right then, even though I was very young, I made a decision: I was going to save my first kiss for my wedding!

I'm sure you've noticed that it is common for girls to be pairing off with boys by the time they are in kindergarten. By middle school their lives seems to be wrapped around dating and boyfriends. I have often thought how sad it is that girls treat so lightly the things that could be so precious. Your first kiss is one of the most valuable gifts you can give. Save it. Treasure it.

THE CAKE

Suppose you made a beautiful birthday cake. It was a rich chocolate cake with homemade vanilla frosting. You spent all afternoon taking the time to make sure it was flawless. You decorated it carefully with frosting, flowers, leaves, and lettering, and added a few cherries for the final touch. Then, enjoying the aroma of a freshly baked chocolate cake, you left it on the counter so that it would be ready for the birthday party.

Then suppose I came along, saw the cake, and feeling a little hungry, decided to cut a piece for myself. Just as I was eating my last bite, you returned to the counter and found your beautiful cake—with a piece missing. So much for all your work making sure each detail of every flower looked perfect. As far as you are concerned, the cake is ruined. There's not time to make a new one. How will it look when you serve it at the party? After all your meticulous work to make it just perfect, how would you feel about my careless attitude?

What if I suggested that you bake another piece of cake to fill in the empty space? Obviously, my advice would irritate you even more.

"Of course not," you'd say. "The cake is ruined. It will never look the same again."

A Proverbs 31 woman will do her husband good, not evil, **all** the days of her life (Prov. 31:12). One of the best ways that you can do good to your future husband today, even if you don't know him yet, is by protecting your heart so that it will be completely his. Your heart is a priceless treasure that you are saving for one. How will your future husband feel if you have already given pieces of your heart to others and can offer him only a partly-eaten cake? He wants a cake baked just for him, not one with pieces missing that others have tasted first. He wants the whole thing—not just part. One day you will long to give him your whole heart—but in order to *give* it later, you must *protect* it now.

EMOTIONAL PURITY

Being reserved for one includes not only physical purity but emotional purity as well. This requires guarding our hearts, our minds, our thoughts, our words, our emotions, and our eyes. It means saving that close, intimate friendship for one man only, avoiding premature emotional attachments, and staying free from the intimate bonds that can form so easily, but are then painful to dissolve. Emotional purity includes guarding our eyes from those "fun" romantic glances and stares, keeping our hearts from being poured out until the right time, and taking captive thoughts that want to run wild with fantasies and dreams.

We see this concept throughout the Bible. Holiness means "being reserved for one." A powerful picture and important pattern is found in Genesis 24:16 where Rebekah reserves herself for Isaac the way the church does for Christ.

Emotional purity is hardly even considered *possible* in our present society. But think of it this way: How would your future husband feel if he knew that some other guy had known your deepest thoughts, dreams, fears, and emotions? What would he think if some other man had known you even better than he himself knows you? Or how would you like it if some other girl had dozens of long, deep, intimate conversations with your husband and knew practically everything there was to know about him?

You see, there is more than just your first kiss and your physical purity that you can save. There are many other "firsts" that will be very special if you *make* them special by saving them for the right time rather than trying to generate romance with every young man you get to know. Sure, most girls your age treat all these things casually. Sure, they might be having fun now, but how is it going to affect their marriages later? Think how meaningful each of these "firsts" can be, when shared with that special someone:

- First expression of interest
- First words of affection or love
- First gift given or received
- First romantic look into his eyes
- First trip together
- First special song, place, event, or memory
- First ring
- First dinner date
- First personal letter expressing emotions
- First "I love you"
- First piece of your heart given
- First serious or ongoing correspondence with a young man
- First special affectionate nicknames or actions
- First kiss

This is not by any means a list of rules—rather, it's a list to make you think. Many young people seem to want to get as close to "the line" as possible and still remain pure. But looking at the big picture of our lives ought to motivate us to have the opposite perspective. The question is not "how little" can I save for my future husband and still be pure—the question is how *much* can I save for him, how many little special and meaningful "firsts" will I have to share with him? It is not that we are merely trying to avoid the worst, but rather that we desire to achieve the best!

Be thou rescued only once.

THE GIFT

Suppose that one day you are summoned by the king and entrusted with an important assignment. You are given a gift. But this gift is not for you to keep; rather, it is for you to give away. In order to fulfill your assignment properly, your gift must be given to the right person, at the right time, and in the right way. Until then you must keep it safe, untarnished, and in perfect condition. This assignment is actually quite difficult, for the gift is easily damaged—it can be ruined by the slightest mishandling. This would greatly disappoint both the king and the recipient. Not only must you guard your gift to keep it undamaged, but you must also be careful not to give your gift to the wrong person—to someone of your own choosing rather than the one who meets the king's requirements. Yet another danger is that of presenting the gift to the right person but at the wrong time. So you determine to guard this gift with utmost care and to fulfill the king's assignment perfectly.

But then, what if someone comes along to whom you would like to give your gift? "Maybe there is a chance he could be the right one?" you may think. "Perhaps it would be okay just to let him hold it?"

However, you then remember the importance of your assignment. "No," you insist, "he has no right to take what does not belong to him!" You continue to faithfully keep your gift.

Next, suppose you begin to notice that many servants have been given similar assignments. And instead of guarding their gifts carefully, you find that they are always talking about them, comparing notes, and even sharing with each other the unique treasures entrusted to them. Suppose also that most of them did not think there was anything wrong with this at all, and talked about the great thrill and enjoyment there was in sampling the king's gift. Though the commandment to protect and conceal the gift was clear, only a few honored this command—and these few were often laughed at and looked down upon by others.

In spite of all the negative peer pressure, by God's grace, there is one young man who continues to guard his gift. Then, at last, he finally finds the person for whom his gift is intended—you! With joy and great anticipation he looks forward to the coming exchange (because in the king's loving and perfect plan he had prearranged the two of you to be carrying each other's gift). It is a joyous conclusion to a great adventure.

But it could have been tragically different. What if you had yielded to the temptation to share your gift with others? How would this special one to whom your gift belonged respond if he discovered that, though he had saved his gift for you, you had given your gift to another? How would he feel if the gift had been sampled, shown, defiled, and given away? And suppose, in addition, you had already received a gift from someone else. His would hardly now be a gift. It certainly would have lost all surprise and intrigue. It would no longer be special to you. So he has nothing to receive and not even anything to give.

What exactly is this "gift?" It is "the first time." It is all the many different assortments of "first times" that are part of a romantic love relationship that God brings together for marriage. "First times" are special, but a "first time" occurs only once. This gift is also called *purity*. Purity is destroyed by the premature use of "first times," and with it is lost the very best gift one can ever give to a spouse.

Sorry will be the maiden who hast been rescued by other knights before the coming of Prince Charming.

DOES IT BELONG TO YOU?

Many young people have questions regarding affection. They want to know is "such and such" a kind of affection okay. However, the question they really ought to be asking is this: "Does this affection *belong* to me?" If they are not married, the answer is no. It is not theirs to give or theirs to receive. It does not belong to them.

Did you know that we do not own ourselves? We belong to two individuals: to God and our mate, or our future mate (I Cor. 6:19–20, 7:4). If a girl kisses a boy to whom she is not married, she is taking what does not belong to her and giving away what is not hers to give. In that sense, it is actually theft. She is stealing from him, from his future wife, from her future husband, and from God—and he is stealing from her, from her future husband, from his future wife, and from God. It is a multiple theft. The Bible calls this defrauding (I Cor. 7:1, I Thess. 4:1–7).

Defrauding is deceiving or taking advantage of someone. Young people do it all the time in their dating relationships. For example, Daniel thinks Christy is a really cute girl, so he talks with her every week at church. He winks at her, laughs at her, pats her on the back, flirts with her, and always goes out of his way to stand by her or give her attention. He's not seriously interested in her. In fact, Daniel actually has another girlfriend, but he enjoys the admiration Christy gives him and considers her a nice friend. Christy, on the other hand, is flattered by his attention and is falling more in love with him each time they talk. She thinks about him all week long and is just waiting for the day he will ask her out or express his love. As you can see, she is headed for disappointment. Consider the deep hurt she will feel when she finds out that he intends their relationship to be only a casual friendship. He is defrauding her. Daniel's attitude is purely selfish and less than honest as he enjoys the attention Christy gives to him without considering how the relationship is hurting her.

We as young ladies do exactly the same thing. We are flattered when a young man gives us attention and are often tempted to lead

Pursue not thou another knight's maiden.

him on even when we know we'd never be interested in marrying him. Defrauding can also take place when we dress in a way to get attention for ourselves. We most likely don't intend any harm to guys; we're simply following the patterns of the world. Yet many of the fashions of the world are sensual and immodest. By dressing immodestly and causing him to notice us, we are stirring up desires in him that we are not able to righteously fulfill. This is defrauding. It is selfish. It is the opposite of true love.

THE BIGGER PICTURE

"How about a pumpkin 'n spice latte?" I suggested to Grace as we looked up at the menu.

"Mmm … Or a cappuccino?" she replied.

"I love coffee shops!" I said.

"Me too," Grace agreed. "I think I could live here."

We actually only drink coffee once in a while. But nothing quite compares to the aroma of coffee, a hot drink, a sweet pastry, and, of course, fellowship with someone you love. Grace and I especially like to stop at coffee shops on snowy winter days, sit by the window, watch the snowflakes fall, and enjoy a rich, warm drink.

"So, what should we get, Sarah?"

"I guess I'll order a café mocha," I said, ignoring the fact that I'm sensitive to caffeine. "I'll ask for an extra cup and we'll share it. I just hope this doesn't keep me awake tonight. It's already late afternoon."

"Don't forget to ask for extra whipped cream!" said Grace.

The drink was delicious, but that night as I climbed into bed I was not at all tired. (Caffeine has a big effect on me ☺.) After lying awake for a couple of hours I got to thinking, "I shouldn't have had so much caffeine. Now I'm going to be tired tomorrow."

This has happened more than once. I've gone to a restaurant or bagel shop late in the day and ordered a coffee or cappuccino—knowing full well that caffeine often keeps me awake when bedtime rolls around. True, the cappuccino tastes great, but it's still not worth the consequence of lying awake for several hours and being tired the next day. Somehow I seem to easily forget about the future when ordering my coffee in the afternoon.

You see, we humans frequently make the mistake of basing our actions on our present feelings rather than thinking of the future outcome. Lying awake in bed is not a huge problem (it gives you time to pray). But consider the truly serious decisions with lifelong consequences that also face us. Young people often give up so much for so little. They sacrifice their most valuable treasures for a few moments of fun. If only they would step back for a minute and look at the big picture. If only they would think about the future! Opening your presents early spoils the surprises of Christmas Day. Snacking before the meal ruins the Thanksgiving dinner. Reading the last chapter first spoils the book. Do you want "Mr. Right" or "Mr. Right Now"? Will you choose $1.00 now or $10,000.00 later? Amazingly, most choose the $1.00 now.

Grace was thrilled one morning, a number of years ago, when Grandpa brought over a carton of huge, sweet strawberries just for her. She didn't want to simply gobble them down; she wanted to enjoy them to the utmost. This meant that she needed to figure out the very best location to eat them. Soon Grace had the perfect idea—a tree! "It'll be the *best*," she exclaimed. "How could anyone enjoy a strawberry more than from the top of a tree?"

However, now she faced a problem. How was she supposed to get up there with a strawberry? She needed both hands to climb the tree, so holding a strawberry in one hand was not exactly a possibility. She couldn't think of a way to hold them with her feet—especially since she would need her feet for climbing too. "Hmmm, maybe my mouth would work," she reasoned.

So if you were at our house that summer afternoon, you would have seen a cute eight-year-old girl attempting to climb a large tree with a huge strawberry sticking out of her mouth. She looked rather like a chipmunk. But if you had waited, you would have learned that work gets its rewards.

Soon there she was sitting comfortably up in the tree slowly taking precious bites of her delicious strawberry. "Boy, do I know how to enjoy food!" Grace declared. Afterward, she thought it was so nice she did it all over again!

If enjoying a strawberry can be this much fun, think about the other areas of life that can be so special if enjoyed at the right time and in the right way. It takes some effort and a lot of patience, but the rewards are worth it.

But Can It Be Done?

Is purity possible? Absolutely! God always gives the power and strength to fulfill His commands. I continue to meet more and more happily married couples who have saved their "firsts" for marriage—their first kiss, even their first touch. Every couple I talk to says the same thing: "It was worth the wait."

A friend of mine was engaged to a godly man. She had met him on the mission field, and they were committed to serving the Lord together. Once, during their courtship, the two of them planned to meet in the home of some fellow missionaries. The couple hadn't seen each other for quite some time, so the missionaries had their camera ready, waiting to snap a picture of their kiss when they were reunited. But all they did was joyously greet each other—without a hug or anything! You see, the two of them had committed to saving their first kiss and all physical affection for their marriage. They hadn't even held hands yet. This young man and woman came to visit us just a few months before their wedding and it was obvious—they were definitely in love. Their sparkling eyes gave it away. Seeing the joy in their marriage a short time later confirmed to me the blessings of saving all physical affection for marriage.

I'd like to explain one more thing about the purpose of purity. I have already mentioned how the pain and heartache that frequently result from dating and breaking up can often be avoided by an understanding of God's way and a willingness to wait. Yet, this must not be the ultimate purpose for our commitment to purity. Our goal in life should not be simply to avoid pain.

Our primary motivation must be to please God. Immorality is sin. We must have a resolute commitment to purity because God commands it (I Cor. 6:18–20). We will stand before Him one day and give account of our lives here on earth. Is not our deepest desire to be pleasing to Him? Therefore, it is ultimately our heavenly Bridegroom, not an earthly one, for whom we are keeping ourselves pure.

The second reason we should desire purity is not to *avoid* loss, but to *achieve* gain. Of course it's difficult. But think of what you will gain. Imagine the rewards. Here are just two of the incredible treasures attained by purity:

1. The conditions for the very best marriage!
2. A powerful testimony! In this generation of darkness, you will be a shining example of the purity God intends. Your bright light will not go unnoticed.

What if I Already Messed Up?

"It's too late for me," many girls say. "I've already ruined my life. I could never have the kind of marriage you're talking about. I gave up any hope of that long ago."

This is one of the most common feelings girls struggle with. But there is good news—incredible news. With God all things are possible. The God we serve is a God of forgiveness and a God of second chances. He is able to heal the deepest wounds and to change the hardest hearts. Many who have failed but who have truly and fully repented of their sin are now the ones who have the strongest testimonies and the most powerful life messages to others. I know a number of couples who, despite many past scars, have wonderful marriages today.

The Bible is full of examples of men and women who failed miserably but experienced God's forgiveness and went on to become great heroes of the faith. Let's look at a few.

Think of the woman who was caught in adultery. Jesus did not condemn her but offered her hope—if she repented. Remember His words: *"Go, and sin no more"* (Jn. 8:1–11).

Consider the Samaritan woman who met Jesus at the well. She lived in immorality, going from man to man. Yet when she came to Christ and her life was changed, she had a powerful testimony for the Lord. *"And many of the Samaritans of that city believed on Him for the saying of the woman, which testified, He told me all that ever I did"* (Jn. 4:39). Who knows? This woman may have gone from being the town outcast to being the most godly, respected woman in town. Many Samaritans came to Christ because of her words.

Then there was Mary Magdalene, out of whom Jesus cast seven demons. Demon possession is often accompanied by serious immorality. Did Mary Magdalene become a woman of God? Can there be any doubt? All of church history knows her testimony. Was she acceptable to God? One of the best. In the gospels, the accounts of her faith, devotion, and understanding outshine even that of the disciples (Jn. 20:1–18).

Bathsheba, a beautiful young woman, was certainly under great pressure and temptation when approached by King David himself, the spiritual leader in Israel (II Sam. 11). In this moment of temptation, she yielded and was the tool of the enemy to bring great calamity into David's life. Nevertheless, despite her initial moral failure, there is evidence of true and lasting repentance in the life of Bathsheba. First of all, we know that she was Solomon's teacher (Prov. 1:8; 4:3–4). That's a pretty good credential. God also chose her son to be king. Yet, she has an even greater credential that demonstrates God's mercy, grace, and power to change a person's life. She is the one God used to write Proverbs 31. The author is King Lemuel, a symbolic name for Solomon, which means "Belonging to God." Chapter 31 records what his mother taught him. Listen to Bathsheba's words to Solomon as recorded by Solomon himself in verses 2–3: *"What, my son? and what, the son of my womb? and what, the son of my vows? Give not thy strength unto women, nor thy ways to that which destroyeth kings."* Are not these the words of one who has repented and who, because of the serious consequences she had to face in her life, now hates the sin of immorality and has come to a mature godliness and a true zeal for purity? She had learned very painfully—her first son died. But she repented, humbled herself, and became a godly woman. God then used her convictions to give the world a wonderful chapter of the Bible. What an incredible life message.

One of the most amazing stories is that of Rahab (Josh. 2–6). Here was a woman who was a Canaanite harlot in the city of Jericho. You can't ruin your life much more than that. But when she heard what God was doing in Israel, she didn't have the same reaction as the rest of her countrymen. They feared Israel. She feared God. She demonstrated her faith and spared the spies at the risk of her own life. As a result, when the city of Jericho was destroyed, Rahab and her father's house were spared. Not only was she protected, but she later married a man in Israel named Salmon, and she lived a godly life. But don't stop here; there's more to the story.

Do you remember the account of Ruth? She, too, was a foreigner, but she feared God, abandoned the gods of her country, and was a woman of outstanding faith and character. God gave her one of the most godly and most respected men around for a husband—Boaz. He was a pillar of righteousness in Bethlehem. He would become the great-grandfather of King David. Do you know who this man, Boaz, was? According to Matthew 1:5, he was the descendant of Rahab and Salmon! God raised up Rahab from being a rejected pagan harlot to the top spot in Israel—the royal line. She has the amazing privilege of being part of the genealogy of Jesus Christ!

The Lord loves to take those who are weak, needy, poor, and inadequate, and raise them up for His important purposes. As we have seen from these women from Scripture, God is always ready to forgive, heal, and rebuild the lives of any who turn to Him. We can be cleansed by Christ and be useful in His kingdom. *"Therefore if any man be in Christ, he is a new creature: old things are passed away; behold, all things are become new"* (II Cor. 5:17). This does not mean that there will not be painful corrections and lasting scars, but there can be joy, freedom, and peace in our lives, marriages, and ministry as we are cleansed by Christ and His Word.

What is required for this restoration to take place? Repentance. God is looking for those who have the attitude of the prodigal son and humbly cry to Him saying, "I have sinned. I was wrong. I am unworthy." Come in complete humility to Christ, knowing how you have grieved Him by your sin and that you deserve nothing. Purpose to turn away from sin completely. Purpose to obey immediately.

TOOTH DECAY

Why do you think God allows tooth decay? One reason is that it is a physical example of the spiritual decay that we see all around us. Toothaches hurt! It is especially painful to dig out the decay, but in order to fix the tooth you can't just put in a filling. You've got to dig out the decay first. Painful? That's for sure! But necessary? Absolutely. If you don't take care of the decay, you'll end up with a root canal later (or end up being toothless!)

Many times in our lives we want to heal the toothache, but we're not willing to dig out the decay. We're not willing to confess sin, ask for forgiveness, and make restitution. But we can't expect to move forward spiritually if we have not worked through our unresolved problems. Clearing up past sin always has to be the first step. Digging out tooth decay is painful and miserable, but there is no other way to heal the tooth. And do you know what makes it even more difficult? The most important thing when digging out decay is that you get *all* of it.

I encourage you to get alone with the Lord and examine your life for any decay that needs to be removed. If you have been believing lies of the enemy, repent and replace them with the truth found in God's Word. If you have been harboring bitterness, discontentment, fear, unforgiveness, or wrong attitudes in your heart, repent and ask the Lord for cleansing. If there are polluting influences or habits that are contaminating your life or leading you astray, lay aside every weight and flee from the sin that so easily entangles (Heb. 12:1). If there are people you have hurt (maybe even young men from past dating relationships), go back to them and ask forgiveness. Purpose also that you will one day ask forgiveness of your future husband. If there is sin you've been hiding from your parents, confess it.

To be a vessel the Lord can fully use, our relationship with Him must be unhindered. We are in a spiritual war. The enemy is prowling around as a hungry lion seeking those he might destroy. We must be on our guard, allow no compromise, and seek His best in every area.

I'm writing this book believing that you are one who has chosen the way of wisdom. Proverbs exhorts us that it is beneficial to instruct those who are wise because, even though it is difficult, they will be able to receive instruction and increase in wisdom. Remember also that the Lord never fails to give us the strength to carry out what He has called us to do.

Make a commitment that from this day forward you will keep yourself pure as a clean vessel of Jesus Christ. He is waiting for you to come to Him. He is ready to forgive and cleanse. He knows the plans He has for you—to bless you and to give you a hope and a future (Jer. 29:11, Rom. 8:32).

SUGGESTED MEMORY VERSE:

"For this is the will of God, even your sanctification, that ye should abstain from fornication: that every one of you should know how to possess his vessel in sanctification and honor" (I Thessalonians 4:3–4).

SUGGESTED ASSIGNMENT:

As you encounter various types of people at church, work, school, or other activities, you will likely get questions from individuals who want to know if you are dating, if you have a boyfriend, and if not, why you don't. Rather than feeling intimidated by the questions you receive, think of this as an opportunity to share with others some of the things the Lord has taught you. It is helpful if you prepare answers to these questions in advance. How can you teach Biblical concepts without offending others or coming across that you think you're better than they are? Get out a piece of paper, ask the Lord for wisdom, and write out your answers to several of the most-asked questions. *"But sanctify the Lord God in your hearts: and be ready always to give an answer to every man that asketh you a reason of the hope that is in you with meekness and fear"* (I Pet. 3:15).

Here are some sample questions:

- When are you going to find a boyfriend?
- How will you ever get to know someone if you don't date?
- How will you know he is the right one if you've never dated anyone else?
- What is so wrong with kissing now?

When Peer Pressure Attacks

TESTIMONY BY A YOUNG LADY

I was your typical Christian homeschooled girl. I went to church all my life and had been taught what was right and wrong. I read my Bible and believed what it said, but it never fully set in. I did not have an intimate relationship with my heavenly Father.

When I was about thirteen, I began to have some problems at home. I couldn't get along with my mom. I felt like I was missing out on the real world. Life with my family was a constant battle. So finally my mom gave up on me and enrolled me in public school. I had no idea what I was in for.

Up until that point, I thought I had strong convictions about dating, language, and other areas of life. My convictions lasted for about two days, and then I started to question everything I had been brought up believing. I was mad at the world for the way my life was going, and I decided to give up on God. I wasn't going to trust Him with my life anymore. As far as I was concerned, God had done a good job of messing up my life and now I was going to fix it on my own.

The pressure to conform to peers, have a boyfriend, and to party with friends started the minute I walked in the door of my school. At first I was determined not to yield to temptation. Several guys asked me out, but I refused. Yet the more I said no to the invitations to parties, dates, and proms, the more I wanted to give in. I wished I could just do what everyone else was doing. One day in English class a young man invited me out on a date. I said no, but then I kicked myself afterwards. I wanted to say yes so badly, yet I also knew it went against what I believed.

My relationship with God was hanging by a thread and slipping away faster and faster as the school year passed. My convictions were smothered by the thoughts and influences that surrounded me everyday at school. All I wanted was to be happy and to have fun, but instead I felt so unhappy and unfulfilled. I was on a downward spiral, allowing my life to be ruled by the impulse of my flesh and the desire to have fun *now*.

The guy from my English class didn't give up very easily. He got a job at the place I was working over the summer, and we began to spend more and more time together. I began to look to him to meet my emotional needs. After a few weeks we were inseparable. I gave a big part of myself to him both physically and emotionally, and never stopped to think about what I was doing. He was a nice guy, and he said he was a Christian, but I knew he was not God's best for my life.

Then one day my boyfriend asked me to marry him. This really made me stop and think. My life was a mess. All I was living for was fun. I had no true joy. Running my life myself was not working as well as I had planned. My relationship with God had become last on my list of priorities. How could God take me back after all that I had done?

I struggled as I wondered whether or not I should marry this young man. I knew that I had fallen away from God. I knew that the Lord had something better in store for my life. I desperately wanted to say yes to my boyfriend, but I couldn't. Looking back, I know it was God's grace that gave me the strength to say no, and after a few weeks we broke up. I was hurt, sad, and lost. I felt used and dirty.

Finally, one night I prayed and told the Lord, "I know I don't deserve Your mercy or forgiveness, but if You will take me back, I will be Yours." I asked the Lord to give me a desire for Himself and to take control of my life. It's not that everything changed overnight. But as I obeyed the Lord, I slowly began to feel God's peace. I began to experience true happiness. With God there is lasting peace and joy that you can't find anywhere else—not with a guy, parties, or friends. God is always there, ready to forgive us no matter what we have done. Often when I realize the incredible love and forgiveness of my heavenly Father, all I can do is fall on my knees in tears and thank Him for His goodness to me. By Christ's grace, I have committed to keeping myself pure for my future husband from this day forward.

CHAPTER ELEVEN

Delighting in the Lord

*"Delight thyself also in the Lord; and He shall
give thee the desires of thine heart."*
Psalm 37:4

"Excuse me! You, up on the bridge, I wish to speak with you," the
alligator called out as he swam toward the bridge.

"Oh, it's you. Greetings," said the princess. She looked elegant
today with a white flower in her hair, weaved into her braided crown.

"Thou hast been ignoring me recently," complained the alligator.
"How fares it with thee of late?"

*"I have had a wonderful day enjoying a relaxing time in the garden
and a pleasant stroll through the woods."*

*"And what causes your radiant smile this evening? Let me guess.
Did a special someone send thee flowers today? Or maybe thou hast
changed thy mind about Sir Eloquence?"*

"Oh, yes, a special Someone did send me flowers today. They were so lovely! The roses were so fragrant, the lilies so white, the morning glories so delicate."

"Love sick," muttered the alligator to himself. "I guess I should not be surprised. The first time a girl gets flowers she always goes a bit crazed."

"Actually," the princess continued, "He had sent them before, but I did not realize that they were for me. He sends me flowers nearly everyday now—everyday I take the time to notice them, that is."

"So tell me," inquired the alligator. "When did you meet your special someone?"

"Oh, I have known Him a very long time," the princess replied, "but I am getting to know Him better each day. Today, in fact, we had a very lovely time together."

"You saw him today, then?"

"Well, no, but I talked with Him and He talked with me. I thanked Him for His love. I reminded Him that my life is committed to Him and that my heart belongeth to Him."

"Thou art engaged, then?" he asked.

"Well, yes! I guess so!" she exclaimed.

"When will the wedding be?"

"That is for Him to decide. But He will come for me when everything is ready," she stated.

"But when did you last see him?" the alligator probed.

"I have never seen Him."

"What? Thy father hath arranged thy marriage?"

"Oh, no! I have pledged my love to Him of my own free will," she said joyfully.

"Pledged thy love to a man thou hast never met?"

"Yes, for He has won my heart."

"Well then, he must be quite the hero," the alligator replied cynically.

"Indeed, the greatest hero ever! None compare with Him in valor or power. I love to read of His victorious deeds."

"So he has written to you then?"

"Yes! The most wonderful love letter you could ever imagine. I only wish I knew how to treasure it more."

"But how can you be so sure of his love for you?" he asked.

"He is One who loves not only in word, but also in deed. You see, He paid the ultimate price for me—He gave His life."

"His life?"

"Yes. He died—for me," she said.

"Then thy lover is dead?" the alligator asked.

"Nay, but living. He conquered death," she replied.

"My starry-eyed friend, I fear that thou art more disillusioned than the girl who kissed the frog in hopes it would become a prince."

"Nay, but more sensible than ever before," the princess insisted.

"This is ridiculous," he argued. "All your life you refuse to even socialize with the numerous prospects who would have been delighted to get to know you, and now you insist on marrying a man whom you have never even met or been with?"

*"Oh, but I **have** been with Him! That is the cause for the joy you see. Just today we walked together in the garden and I read again part of His love letter to me. I've been realizing that He has often been waiting for me there, and yet I have repeatedly disappointed Him. I so frequently forget that He loves to hear my voice and to listen to me pour out my heart."*

"May I ask, my love-struck lady, what be his name?"

"He is a Prince, just as I have always dreamed of ... a Prince of Peace. He is the Fairest of Ten Thousand, the Bright and Morning Star, the Alpha and Omega, the Light of the World—"

"Slow down, dear girl. In thy excitement thou art leaving me quite confused."

"Oh, but He is much more," she continued excitedly. "He is my Redeemer, my Fortress, my Deliverer, my Rock, my Shepherd, my Portion, my Strong Habitation, my Banner, my Shield, my Strength, my Hiding Place, my Comfort, my All."

"Oh my, oh my. I had heard that young ladies go crazy when they fall in love, but I never expected it to be like this," mumbled the alligator, splashing the water with his tail.

"You always told me that I was waiting for a dream that would never come true. How foolish I was to listen to you. How foolish to forget that I was not waiting at all," the princess said.

"Not waiting? Then thou hast lied to me all along?"

"Nay, but thou hast lied to me!" she responded. "You told me I could not be happy without a prince; you told me that I would always be alone. Nothing could be further from the truth. What I have been wanting all along, I already have! My greatest dream has already come true. I am already loved with a deeper love than is possible anywhere else."

"It is true," she continued, "that my Prince has asked me to wait for marriage on earth. But He reminded me today that my focus must not be on the waiting, but rather on Himself. Now I see that I never could have been happy with an earthly prince until I had learned what it was to be happy with my real Prince."

"This is nonsense—utter nonsense," muttered the alligator.

"You say you do not understand?" she asked. "Then never mind. Few people do. Few understand what life is truly about. In seeking what is temporary, they lose what is eternal. In searching for only what they can see, they miss out on the unseen—and the unseen is the most real of all."

The One Who Is Sufficient

The princess began to learn that the very relationship she longed for, she already had. She was loved deeply with an everlasting love, and her Prince was waiting with His arms open. The world does not know or comprehend what it is to be in love with Jesus. Few understand that our greatest joy in life will come from fulfilling that purpose for which we were created—having fellowship with our Creator and glorifying Him (Rev. 4:11).

Marriage on earth is only a picture of the spiritual relationship that the Lord wants to have with every one of us. Anything we desire in marriage, we have completely in the Lord. We long for someone who loves us, understands us, listens to us, provides for us, protects us, cares for us—is crazy about us! God gives these desires. Don't you think the One who instills the desires knows how to fulfill them? In every one of these ways, the Lord is far more able to meet our needs than anyone on earth ever could.

AN EARTHLY PICTURE

Here is a partial list of the ways that the marriage relationship parallels and pictures the relationship God designed for us to have with Christ:

1. Both relationships are permanent.
2. Both are intimate.
3. Both require waiting—waiting for a wedding, waiting for Christ's return.
4. Both are based on love and commitment.
5. In both, the two become one—husband and wife become one flesh; those who are saved become members of Christ's body (Eph. 5:29–31, Jn. 17:21).
6. Both are covenants and formed by vows.
   Marriage—*"I do"*
   Salvation—*"If thou shalt confess with thy mouth the Lord Jesus"* (Rom. 10:9)
7. Both are exclusive.
   They are not shared by another—no adultery, no idolatry.
8. Both have a starting moment.
   When you are born into the world, you are neither *married* nor *saved*. Marriage requires a ceremony; salvation requires a decision.
9. Both relationships make us complete.
10. Both have a wedding/marriage supper—a wedding banquet on earth, the marriage supper of the Lamb in heaven (Rev. 19).
11. Both are sealed with a sign—marriage with a ring, salvation with the Holy Spirit.
12. Both have an authority structure, a head to the relationship to whom the other desires to submit—the wife submits to her husband as the believer submits to Christ.
13. In both, even though there is an authority structure, the relationship is based on a friendship—*"I have called you friends"* (Jn. 15:15).

14. In both, the groom must leave his home. Christ left His Father in order to come to earth and win His bride. A man will leave his father and mother and cleave to his wife (Eph. 5:31).
15. In both relationships, the head is the initiator.
16. Both require sacrificial love on the part of the head. A husband is commanded to love as Christ loved the church and gave Himself for it (Eph. 5:25).
17. In both, the head is the provider and the protector.
18. In both, the husband prepares a residence—a man provides a home on earth, Christ provides a home in heaven.
19. In both relationships, the bride becomes beautiful by a submissive spirit and inner qualities of godliness (I Pet. 3:1-6).
20. In both, the bride's exclusive desire is to please and serve her head.
21. In both, the bride becomes radiant with joy.
22. Both relationships grow sweeter with time.
23. In both relationships, each owns the other. *"I am my beloved's, and my beloved is mine"* (Song of Sol. 6:3, I Cor. 7:4).
24. In both relationships, each fills the other's heart (Ps. 139:17–18, Col. 1:27).
25. Both relationships provide a "satisfaction" that can be found nowhere else. We are satisfied by a relationship with God and by being in His presence. Likewise, we are satisfied by our spouse, even just by being in their presence.

He Who Sees Our Tears

Grace and I were driving home and discussing our day. We had just finished playing our harps for a ladies' retreat—providing soft background music for their times of prayer and sharing.

"You know," I said to Grace, "most of the ladies who attended this retreat were married, but they still have the same struggles that most singles have. They are still longing for love, admiration, and fulfillment."

"Yes," Grace agreed, "I was thinking the same thing."

During their sharing times, many women had stood up and tearfully shared about the various struggles they were going through.

Some were having problems in their families, health, or friendships, but most were having struggles in their marriages. With heartache, many expressed that their husbands were not providing the spiritual leadership, love, or companionship they desired.

To whom did these ladies turn in their times of need? To the Lord. He was ready to comfort them. He was waiting to provide the love for which they were longing and to meet the needs their husbands couldn't meet for them. You see, even if we are married, the Lord is the only One who can ultimately meet the longings of our hearts. Without being satisfied with our heavenly Prince, we will never be satisfied with an earthly one.

Of course, it's natural to be excited about our future marriage here on earth or to be dreaming about our wedding day and marriage. However, the Lord continually reminds me that I should be most excited about Him—knowing, serving, and being with Him. I should be anxiously awaiting the coming of my true Bridegroom. *"Looking for that blessed hope, and the glorious appearing of the great God and our Savior Jesus Christ"* (Tit. 2:13).

A White Horse

I looked out into the dark parking lot. Our van was way at the other side. I didn't mind the walk, but I wasn't so thrilled about making the trip in the rain. I didn't have an umbrella, but it was time to leave. So I decided to make a dash for it. I gathered my things together and was just about to begin my venture when my brother's cell phone rang. "It's for you, Sarah," he said and handed me the phone. "Hello," I said, as I stepped outside the door and started running. The call was from one of my friends who wanted to share the exciting news that she was engaged! "Congratulations!" I exclaimed, maneuvering my way past cars and trying to hold a bag over my head. "I'm so excited for you!"

The news wasn't too much of a surprise since I knew she was courting—but I wasn't expecting the call to come *quite yet*! Before I went to bed, I sent her a quick e-mail to congratulate her and to say how encouraged I was by her testimony. I said something like, "You were willing to wait upon the Lord and He has blessed you. You stayed in the castle of God's protection—until one day you looked up to see a prince coming on a white horse!"

I was genuinely excited for my friend, but I was also praying that her engagement wouldn't distract me with longings for marriage or with thoughts of discontentment. Only moments after I sent my e-mail, the Lord brought an exciting thought to my mind— "Remember the passage you read this morning, Sarah? Remember the verse you chose as your verse of the day?"

Yes, I remembered! How could I have forgotten? I grabbed my Bible and read it again: *"And I saw heaven opened, and behold a white horse; and He that sat upon him was called Faithful and True, and in righteousness He doth judge and make war"* (Rev. 19:11).

Once again, the Lord was faithful to remind me on that rainy night that He is my bridegroom, and that my greatest joy will always come from my relationship with Him. He is the One I am ultimately waiting for. When I am tempted to feel sorry for myself (such as when friends get engaged), the Lord brings along special little encouragements to remind me that He is in perfect control of my life.

One time I was surrounded by people at a special event. I was smiling, laughing, and chatting, but only the Lord understood how I was actually feeling. Some other friends had just announced their engagement, and the Lord knew I needed an extra reminder to stay focused on Him. So He sent me a special gift. A ten-year-old boy who was a friend of mine came up to me and handed me a flower. He had no idea how I was feeling, but the timing was perfect. I knew that the flower was actually from the Lord. My heavenly Father was telling me to look to Him, to wait for Him, and to remember that He knew exactly what He was doing in my life.

How to Fall in Love With Jesus

SPEND TIME ALONE WITH HIM.

When two people are in love, they never want to be separated. They look for ways to be together. They sacrifice all other interests and ambitions in order to make time for each other. In the same way, we will never experience the joy of falling in love with Jesus unless we make the effort to spend time alone with Him.

Set aside special occasions just to be with the Lord. The princess spent an afternoon in the garden fellowshipping with her heavenly Father. Jesus rose early to pray. Daniel prayed three times a day. Do whatever you must do to arrange this time alone. Pour out your heart to Him in prayer. Be still before the Lord and listen to what He says to you.

"One thing have I desired of the Lord, that will I seek after; that I may dwell in the house of the Lord all the days of my life, to behold the beauty of the Lord, and to inquire in His temple" (Ps. 27:4).

Learn to get to know Him.

When a couple is in love, they want to learn as much as they can about each other. They love to share the details of their day. They find themselves suddenly interested in the other person's interests, and they are delighted to be a part of every area of one another's life.

It brings glory and pleasure to our Maker when we have this same burning desire to get to know Him—when we seek after Him and long to understand His ways. *"Thus saith the Lord, Let not the wise man glory in his wisdom, neither let the mighty man glory in his might, let not the rich man glory in his riches; But let him that glorieth glory in this, that he **understandeth and knoweth Me**"* (Jer. 9:23–24, emphasis added).

Seek to know the ways of the Lord. Learn to love what He loves and to hate what He hates. Be interested in the things He tells you. Never forget that He delights in your prayers and that He is concerned about the smallest details of your life.

Treasure His love letter to you.

Perhaps you have noticed that a girl in love waits anxiously for the mail to arrive, hoping that there might be a special letter for her. This letter is not set aside with the other mail, or read once and filed away. No, it is read, re-read, and treasured.

God's Word is more valuable and precious than any earthly love letter. Read it every day. Re-read it. The letter gets better every time! Memorize it. Meditate on it day and night. Apply it to your life.

"O how love I Thy law! It is my meditation all the day. ... How sweet are Thy words unto my taste! Yea, sweeter than honey to my mouth!" (Ps. 119:97, 103)

Understand what He has done for you.

It is interesting that many cultures have romance stories of a knight who comes to slay the dragon and rescue the princess. This is what Christ did in the greatest love story ever! He defeated Satan, the dragon, when He died on the cross, and He rescued His bride from her captivity to sin (Col. 2:13–15). Soon He will take us to the home that He is preparing for us.

An enormous price was paid by our Rescuer. Christ went from the highest position of glory to the lowest place of humiliation—God's judgment. Not only did Jesus suffer the rejection and pain inflicted by men, but even worse, He bore the wrath of God as our substitute. The just gave His life for the unjust.

Those who trust Christ are pardoned from guilt, exempt from eternal punishment, declared righteous in God's sight, born into His family, given a new nature, promised an inheritance, and granted everlasting life with God. This salvation is a gift. It cannot be earned. *"Who hath delivered us from the power of darkness, and hath translated us into the kingdom of His dear Son: In whom we have redemption through His blood, even the forgiveness of sins"* (Col. 1:13–14).

Frequently tell Him of your love.

Does your heart belong to the Lord? Is your life committed to Him? Is He first place in your life? Tell Him! God loves to hear your voice! Remind Him often of your love and of your desire to always be loyal to Him. Of course He already knows, but tell Him anyway. Talk to Him every chance you get. *"The prayer of the upright is His delight"* (Prov. 15:8).

Demonstrate your love by your actions.

A young lady in love has one goal—to please the one in whom she delights. Her life is centered around making him successful. She is focused on his needs. Her own ambitions are lost in her desire to serve him. She doesn't consider this to be a sacrifice on her part. No, it is her delight.

The Lord Himself has told us, *"My little children, let us not love in word, neither in tongue; but in deed and in truth"* (I Jn. 3:18). If we truly love Him, we will obey His commandments. We will joyfully pour out our lives for His sake, and our deepest desire will be to bring Him glory.

TELL OTHERS ABOUT HIS GREATNESS.

A bride-to-be has trouble talking about anything else besides her fiancé. His name seems to come up in every conversation. After you've spent a little time with her, you feel that you've heard everything there is to hear about this amazing person whom she loves.

Well, we have a lot of exciting information to share about the One who has won our heart! Tell of the Lord's greatness. Declare what He has done for you. Remind others of Christ's credentials. Be excited when you talk of Him! Seek to turn the focus of every conversation to the Lord. If others speak badly of Him, be quick to defend Him.

"My mouth shall show forth Thy righteousness and Thy salvation all the day" (Ps. 71:15).

WORSHIP HIM.

"Give unto the Lord the glory due unto His name; worship the Lord in the beauty of holiness" (Ps. 29:2). Spend time at the feet of Jesus. Worship is simply the act of humbling ourselves before the Lord, expressing our thankfulness, and praising His greatness. It is something done in spirit and in truth, in the quietness of the heart. It is not a meeting or musical experience. Although praise can be expressed in these settings, be careful not to confuse emotion or music with true worship.

Times of worship and adoration will strengthen your relationship with the Lord, satisfy your deepest longings, and give you fresh, new glimpses of His glory and greatness. You will find that in His presence there truly is fullness of joy (Ps. 16:11).

Be attentive to the gifts He gives you.

"Every good gift and every perfect gift is from above, and cometh down from the Father of lights" (Jas. 1:17). Every day the Lord showers us with blessings and gifts that we often take for granted. Take the time to notice His acts of lovingkindness. Give thanks both for the gifts you appreciate and the things you don't understand—knowing that all His gifts are good ones. Post verses or other reminders in your room that will cause you to remember Him throughout the day.

Keep journals of your times together.

Write letters and songs to the Lord. This will enable you to express your thoughts, to creatively tell Him of your love, and to have a record of your times together. Write down the special things He does for you, His answers to prayer, and the lessons He teaches you. We so easily forget about all He has given us. Keep journals to remind you of His faithfulness in the past and of your gratitude to Him.

"Bless the Lord, O my soul, and forget not all His benefits" (Ps. 103:2).

Run into His arms whenever you need comfort.

"Therefore the Lord longs to be gracious to you, And therefore He waits on high to have compassion on you" (Is. 30:18 NASB). *"My soul clings to You; Your right hand upholds me"* (Ps. 63:8 NASB).

Often the struggles, hurts, and trials you encounter are for the specific purpose of directing you to the Lord. He longs to comfort you. His arms are open to you. Learn to run into them and find the love, security, and intimacy for which you long.

Delighting in the Lord is not some make-believe or fanciful idea. It is not something to simply help us "survive" until a husband comes along. Knowing Christ is the real thing. It is the greatest thing. If others do not believe this, it is because they don't know Him well enough yet; they haven't experienced the joy and fulfillment of His presence. Many in the world know *about* the Lord but do not know Him personally as Savior. Yet all who have learned what it is to abide in His presence and to walk in His fellowship, join with the psalmist in saying, *"Whom have I in heaven but Thee? and there is none upon earth that I desire beside Thee"* (Ps. 73:25).

Doubt not the faithfulness of thy heavenly Prince.

SUGGESTED MEMORY VERSE:

"Delight thyself also in the Lord; and He shall give thee the desires of thine heart" (Psalm 37:4).

SUGGESTED ASSIGNMENT:

Have you ever prayed for a whole hour? Find a place where you can be alone without interruptions for an entire hour. If this isn't possible at your home during the day, go to a park, an empty room at your church, or consider getting up in the middle of the night. Spend the hour in communion with the Lord. To help you stay focused, write a schedule for yourself to follow.

Here is a sample pattern you could use:

5 minutes – worship

5 minutes – thanksgiving

5 minutes – confession

5 minutes – pray Psalms to the Lord

5 minutes – pray for your authorities

5 minutes – pray for missionaries

5 minutes – pray for unsaved friends and family

5 minutes – other general requests

5 minutes – ask for wisdom, grace, and humility in specific areas
in which you know you need to change

5 minutes – personal requests

5 minutes – ask for God's abundant blessing

5 minutes – praise and thanksgiving

The Nearness of God

TESTIMONY FROM A YOUNG LADY

As I was reading my Bible toward the end of last December, I was keeping my eyes open for a verse to especially focus on in 2006. Then one morning, I found it—a verse that really summed up my desires for the new year! Psalm 73:28 says, *"But as for me, the nearness of God is my good; I have made the Lord God my refuge, that I may tell of all Your works."* As this verse jumped out at me, I thought to myself, "That is exactly what I want! I want to have such a close relationship with the Lord that I won't be dependant on others to give me joy or satisfaction." I asked the Lord to help me to truly understand what it means to have the nearness of God be my good, and to enable me to seek Him first and to fall in love with my Savior!

As January began, I was excited about the upcoming year and wondering what the Lord would bring into my life to help me grow in this area. Just a few weeks later our family heard some shocking news. A young man from our church told my dad that he was interested in pursuing a relationship with my older sister with the purpose of marriage! My sister joyfully said that she was also interested in him and wholeheartedly agreed to a courtship. This began a whole new chapter of my life! At first I wasn't sure what to think. I was excited for my sister, but I felt like I was losing one of my best friends. Seeing my sister's joy also reminded me of my desire to someday get married and began to stir up thoughts of discontentment. The first week of her courtship was really hard. I was definitely struggling.

Then God reminded me of the verse that I had chosen at the beginning of the year. *"But as for me, the nearness of God is my good."* I knew I needed to look to the Lord—not my sister, nor anyone else—to meet my needs and to be my closest friend.

As soon as I remembered this, I started looking for ways

to use my sister's courtship to help me delight in the Lord. I decided that I would keep a journal to record parallels between my sister's relationship with this young man, and my own relationship with the Lord.

I started to look at my sister's courtship with new excitement. It has been a special reminder to me of how faithful my God is, how much I can trust Him, and how worthy He is of my whole heart!

When the young man first asked my sister if he could get to know her better, she faced the initial shock of, "Wow! He's actually interested in me!" This reminded me of the initial joy and amazement we experience when we first understand that God loves us and wants us to be with Him forever.

Soon my sister was excited to tell everyone the news about her courtship. I should have the same excitement and desire to tell everyone I meet about Christ.

One day the young man who is courting my sister gave her a bouquet of flowers. This caused me to wonder, "How does the Lord send me flowers to show that He cares for me?" I began to think of the many little blessings that He had given me, and I wrote them down in my journal.

Another thing I've noticed is how my sister's face lights up when she talks to or about this young man. This is how I want my relationship with the Lord to be—I want others to see by my countenance the joy that He has brought into my life.

It seems that the more my sister gets to know this young man, the better she finds him to be. This is true a thousand times over when we get to know the Lord. He seems to get better and better! The more you get to know Him, the sweeter He is!

It has been so neat to see how God has been helping me to delight in Him this year through the events of my sister's courtship. I am looking forward to growing closer to Him each day.

CHAPTER TWELVE

Know That God Arranges Marriages

"Now unto Him that is able to do exceeding abundantly above all that we ask or think, according to the power that worketh in us, unto Him be glory in the church by Christ Jesus throughout all ages, world without end. Amen."
Ephesians 3:20–21

"Your Majesty," spoke Sir Gallant, "many knights have taken notice of thy daughter, that she be attractive, mature, friendly and ... and ... and unmarried. Would the king consider hosting a contest to win her hand? A contest for one of the loyal knights of the kingdom to prove himself worthy of her? It would be an event to capture the heart of the whole kingdom, and it would assure thy daughter of the grandest knight to be found—a husband of stature and leadership, something that I know is thy heart's desire."

The king looked intently at the delegation and then paced several times before he spoke. "The king," he said, "most certainly desires the best for his daughter and the qualities of which you speak. What contest would you propose, and how would the champion be determined?"

"Your Majesty, the contest would be open to all the young men of the kingdom. It would not be a small event but would span the sum of three days. An array of games and competitions would be held, including all forms of combat, many skills of the farm and craft, the ability of debate, and a concluding jousting match. Then at a great feast the king himself shall judge and announce the victor."

The delegation waited for the king's response as he thought for a few moments. What would the princess think? Someone who could be champion of the games would certainly be able to protect her, but this would not ensure that his life purpose would be the same as that of the princess. He who showed himself superior in skills of farm and craft would be able to provide for her, but would she love him? The debate would be won by Sir Eloquence. That would not do. And jousting? This would be entertaining and a good jousting match is popular—but would all of this determine God's choice?

Finally the king answered, "I will discuss this and give thee an answer tomorrow."

The evening meal was an interesting time. The servants were intrigued, the princess was resistant, and the queen was horrified. The king just smiled and listened to the multitude of responses. In the morning he gave his answer. "The contest shall be held! But not for the hand of the princess. The victor shall receive a silver sword with a golden hilt. The hand of the princess, however, shall be reserved for the one of God's choosing."

The contest was scheduled for that summer. It became the talk of the kingdom and captured the interest of not a few young men, squires, and knights. Many displayed outstanding talent as they spent hours in practice. In their preparation for the contest, some exhibited their strength, others their skill, and still others their knowledge and leadership.

One humble knight, however, did not plan to participate. He was too focused on other duties and had not the time to prepare. He would have enjoyed the contest, but he knew he was needed elsewhere. Furthermore, he was not seeking recognition or fame.

*   *   *

This same knight of the kingdom was riding alone in early summer along the stone road to the castle. The wind blew through his dark hair as he rode with dignity on his noble white steed. Crossing the bridge over the moat, the knight heard an unexpected voice.

"From whence come ye?"

Looking around, the knight saw the alligator down below. "From yonder villages on the edge of the kingdom," he answered.

"Be ye on important business?" asked the alligator.

"Be ye the castle receptionist?" returned the knight.

"Nay, but a trusted subject of the king who guardeth his domain."

"Yea, I be on important business," replied the knight.

"I hope it be not for the hand of the princess. She is a hopeless case."

"Art thou the dragon guarding her also, whom I must slay to rescue her?"

"Nay again, thou royal knight. I be her friend and wise counselor, if it be not inappropriate to say so of myself. But alas, she refuseth to listen to me."

The knight, unsure whether to feel irritated or entertained, did not respond.

"So then," the alligator asked curiously, "comest thou for the princess?"

"My business, oh wise one, is to report of the battles of the kingdom," the knight answered.

"Battles? Oh my! Have we not peace throughout the borders? This be news to me."

"We have not peace, oh great counselor. I thought thou saidst that thou wast wise. Dragons and giants do roam the land."

"Such news be nonsense," replied the reptile. "Thou art beginning to sound as foolish as the princess. I have not seen a giant in years, though a dragon or two have visited on occasion."

"They have terrorized the land. Much damage hath been done," declared the knight.

"I cannot speak for giants, but I fear that you misjudge dragons. They are often misunderstood," spoke the alligator. "Let them be. They intend no harm."

"Thy words remind me of the evil dragon himself, oh superb analyst. Didst thou at one time live in a garden? I'm pleased to hear that the princess is not taken in by thy words."

After talking more of the princess and hearing some of the alligator's stories, the knight departed from the bridge and entered the castle courtyard. He petitioned a hearing with the king and was subsequently brought into his royal chamber. The king was pleased to see him, and they retreated to a private conference room to discuss the kingdom at length.

"I have not compassion for those who promote ungodly attitudes and who bring moral snares and traps into families and villages," the knight declared.

"The blind leading the blind," the king sighed. "But we must not forget that the true enemy is neither flesh nor blood. Let us not be surprised by his craftiness. He is the father of lies and a prowling lion seeking only to destroy."

"Indeed," said the knight. "He attacks when we least expect it, and I have noticed that young people are often his target."

"Tis true, for they will be the leaders of the next generation," the king replied.

The knight had spoken of these matters with the king many times previously. He did, however, have another purpose for this visit to the king. He had long noticed and thought about the princess and sought, whenever the discussion allowed, to bring questions of her into the conversation as naturally as possible. He had often looked for ways to talk about her without disclosing his personal interest. But he had decided that today was going to be different—it would be a day to speak of the matter more plainly.

"Sire, what thinketh thy daughter of the coming contest?"

"She findeth it only an item of amusement but not of serious interest. The princess knoweth there be war and that we be under siege by an unseen enemy. She hath a heart for the true needs of the kingdom—as

thou also hast, Sir Valiant. She has much work to do and her time is needed elsewhere, in the villages."

Sir Valiant recognized this as an opportunity to pursue the important matter on his heart. He suddenly began talking at a much slower pace, and the king sensed a nervousness in his voice. This was truly a frightening occasion for Valiant, for more was at stake than any single encounter in battle. The king listened with great interest to hear what Sir Valiant was going to say next, and perhaps the king himself was also a little nervous.

"Your Majesty, I would like to speak to thee of another matter of personal business. I know that many young men in the kingdom are interested in the princess. I am not as experienced, skilled, or noble as many other a knight, but if it be not too bold, Sire, I would like to express my own interest in thy daughter. Could it be that thou wouldst consider my request? What wouldst thou require for her hand?"

It was hard for Sir Valiant to believe that he had just spoken these less-than-eloquent words and had actually posed this request to the king himself.

"Why askest thou for her hand?" questioned the king. "Why doth she please thee?"

"Sire, though she be a princess, I have seen no greater servant. And though she be beautiful, she gloweth even more greatly within. And, my lord, though she hath opportunity to meet many a knight, she falleth for none because she seeketh one. I find not, Sire, another maiden in the kingdom that be of such mind, heart, and demeanor."

"Thou hast answered well, Sir Valiant. And not only with thy words, for I have observed also thy loyalty, diligence, faithfulness, and understanding. It would please me to give my daughter and my blessing to such as thyself. I shall talk to the princess and her mother on thy behalf."

The king spoke briefly with the queen, but they needed not a long discussion, for they had spoken of Sir Valiant many times before and had observed his faithful service. They knew of no other young man in the kingdom with his understanding and stature. The queen was delighted, as the king knew she would be. Then the king walked outside to meet the princess.

But How Will It Work for Me?

"How am I ever going to meet someone?" you may wonder. "How will we get to know each other? How will I know he is the right one?"

I have exciting news. No two stories are alike. God has a unique plan—you might call it an adventure—for each individual. It is a journey into the unknown. There are dangers; yet, as we have already discussed, there are also safeguards. An adventure has a clear objective and destination, but the path to get there is uncertain and calls for careful navigation. It requires wisdom, skill, courage, faith, pain, hard work, and patience.

Slay thou the dragon before thou rescuest the princess

Every journey is different and, in the same way, finding the right life partner will be different for everyone. I have no idea where you will meet Mr. Right, how you will get to know him, or even if it is God's will for you to marry at all. But that's what makes it exciting.

You get to watch God's story for your life unfold. There are many unknowns, but God has a plan and the power to carry it out. There's no use trying to guess how it will happen, figure it out in advance, or *help* God bring it to pass. (But remember we should do our part—pray and prepare.) The Lord loves to surprise us! His plan will most likely be different than what you ever expected—but one day you'll be able to look back and see that it was perfect in every way.

Coming Together

Even though God's specific plan will be different for each of us, are there any foundational principles that we can follow? Let's say we meet someone who we believe might be Mr. Right. How do we get to know him? Where do we start?

There is one simple sequence I can give you that applies to everyone. Look carefully at the following chart:

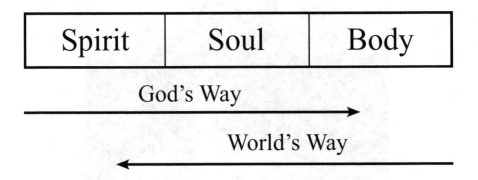

We are spirit, soul, and body. The spiritual and physical are rivals (Gal. 5:16–17). The physical always wants to take charge and control us, but we must not let it dominate—especially in this area of relationships. The joining together of two people in marriage needs to happen in the proper order: spiritual first, physical last. In the American system of dating as we know it today, young people think they can start with the physical. Often such relationships don't even get to the spiritual dimension at all. As you can see from the chart, God's ways and the world's ways are exactly opposite.

Now let's take this concept—of spirit first, then soul, then body—and think about how it might work as we come together with a life partner. Keep in mind that the following suggested sequence is not a formula or a recipe, but simply a general guideline.

Observe

As the Lord brings someone into your path who is of interest to you, your first step is not to show interest or get excited about him, but just to observe. It's good when parents can help with this too. What are his goals? Does he know the Lord? Is there ministry and spiritual fruit in his life? Is he committed to the Word of God? How does he treat his mother and sisters? (See page 77 for more ideas of questions to ask yourself about him.)

Acquainted as Casual Friends

If God desires to bring two people together, He will give opportunities for them to get to know each other in natural settings—at church, school, work, homes of friends, conferences, camps, Christian organizations, ministry projects, or in one of God's other creative match-making situations.

You do not need to date in order to get to know another person. You actually learn more about an individual by seeing him in real life situations. Anybody can act mature, romantic, and considerate on a date. But how does he live in everyday life? How does he interact with people? How does he respond to various stresses and pressures?

Young Man Takes Initiative

When a young man (or a young man's father) expresses interest, a new phase of the adventure suddenly begins. Interest has been specifically *expressed!* Now what?

It is at this point that parents (and/or other godly mentors) can play a key role in screening and protecting our emotions. If parents take the time to get to know a young man first, ask the many important questions, find out where he is spiritually, and discuss how your life goals fit together, think how much parents can determine before we get too emotionally involved. This is a tremendous safeguard for us! I'm not talking about an "arranged" marriage. I'm talking about using common sense to avoid mistakes, pain, and heartache. My parents understand how I think, and they know what I'm looking for in a spouse. I trust them. I trust God to give direction through them. If my parents have "checked out" a guy first, I will feel a whole lot safer in pursuing this serious matter.

Why is it the responsibility of the man to take the initiative? First of all, it is the Biblical pattern. Christ sought the church to be His bride, not vice versa. In Scripture, men *took* wives. Women, on the other hand, were *given* in marriage by their fathers. Since the man is to be the leader and the head of the relationship, it is appropriate for him to take the leadership from the beginning. If a woman initiates the relationship at the start, she may be tempted to continue to lead throughout the marriage. This is clearly not God's design. Man was not created for woman, but woman for man (I Cor. 11:9). The husband is to be the provider and the protector. The woman is his treasured prize! The prize does not seek after the winner, but the winner for the prize.

If the young man meets the qualifications, if you are interested, and if the Lord so directs through His Word and your authorities, now is an opportunity to begin building the friendship. As you proceed, it is best to first continue to get better acquainted in a group setting. I know one family that simply has a particular "interested" young man come to their home several times a week for supper and just to be with the family. The whole family is getting to know him well.

If possible, it would be nice for the two families to spend some time together as well. In fact, it would be ideal if both families could become good friends and possibly have ministry together.

Close Friendship

This next phase is an exciting part of the adventure—but one still requiring much discernment, caution, and patience. It is tempting to rush ahead at this stage, rather than taking enough time to get to know each other well in a not-too-romantic environment. As much as is possible, the goal is to keep your emotions in check until you determine that this is indeed the life partner God has for you.

It will not be possible for you to successfully make it through this period without your own personal convictions already being in place. No one can *give* you convictions. You must embrace them as your own so that you are firm and steadfast in your commitments and understanding. If not, you'll never have the strength to maintain the purity God desires.

When these convictions *are* in place, it is not necessary to have a formula or a lot of rules set by others. But it would be wise for the two young people to prayerfully determine some kind of framework and guidelines regarding how to handle their time together before marriage.

Solid Christian oversight throughout this time is also extremely valuable. If we are wise, we will desire and seek out counsel and accountability from parents and other godly mentors. God has provided them to help us. We will receive great blessings as we maintain close communication with our parents and welcome their guidance and instruction. It would be especially beneficial to seek their direction as to when it is the right time to progress to each new step of the relationship.

Allow this phase to take as much time as is necessary. It is important to get to know each other well. We accomplish this not just by *being* together, but by *doing* together. Choose specific ministry projects that the two of you can work on as a team.

There are also many areas that will be important to discuss during this courtship period: your purpose in life, your future ministry goals, your doctrine, your convictions, your views of family and child raising, and your spiritual walk. But it is still best to avoid intimate talks until there is official engagement.

Engagement

Engagement is the home stretch toward marriage. Many long talks have already occurred, but ahead are some of the most special times and a greater level of intimacy as you enjoy a new sense of belonging to one another. A couple needs plenty of time together in order to have those necessary long talks that engagement requires.

But you still do not want to put yourselves in any tempting situations. There are lots of opportunities to be together while just going about normal daily activities. Continue to maintain close accountability with your parents, and purpose to avoid even the appearance of evil.

As explained in the previous chart, the union needs to be built on the foundation of spiritual oneness. Your close bond will become stronger and deeper as you grow together in the Lord and share times of intimacy with Him. Spend time together in the Word and in prayer. Perhaps you would want to have daily devotions together.

Concentrate on the spiritual and continue to wait for the physical. I respect many couples I know who have chosen to reserve their first kiss for their wedding and all physical affection for marriage.

Marriage

In God's amazing plan, the *two* become *one*. As women, we were created to be our husbands' helpmeets. We need to remind ourselves frequently that our purpose in getting married is not to get, but rather to give. We can be assured that, as we follow God's calling and honor His design, His plan is what will bring us ultimate fulfillment and joy.

BUMPS IN THE ROAD

As each of us considers this process of coming together with a future husband, I want to remind you that our primary motivation for caution and wisdom is not to avoid pain. Yes, we do want to avoid *unnecessary* pain—the kind that results from the dating system. And yes, we can avoid many scars and enter marriage as pure individuals if we learn to make wise decisions. But even so, struggles will always be a part of life. God allows many different types of difficulties and hardships to occur, and uses them for His good purposes. *"It is good for me that I have been afflicted; that I might learn Thy statutes"* (Ps. 119:71).

So, I'm not saying that there won't be any struggles or bumps in the road along the way. Rather, I'm saying that out of our love for the Lord and our desire to be obedient to Him, we need to evaluate how we handle each area of life. We want to honor Christ in the way we conduct ourselves and represent Him through this new adventure. Our ultimate goal isn't to avoid struggle, but to glorify the Lord and to be the best wife we can possibly be.

BACK TO THE HERE AND NOW

Romance is a gift from God. Part of the excitement of romance is the unknown and the anticipation. The Lord does not tell us what our future holds. We may know that He has given us specific goals and called us to various assignments, but we do not know the details of how everything will fit together. That is where faith, wisdom, and obedience come into the picture. God doesn't usually show us distant details. He gives a glimpse of the horizon and then just enough light to take the next step.

What next step should we take as we wait to meet Prince Charming? First of all, we should be preparing ourselves to be future wives, and secondly, we should be focusing on our present ministry assignments.

Prepare

In II Timothy 2:20–21 we are told, *"But in a great house there are not only vessels of gold and of silver, but also of wood and of earth; and some to honor, and some to dishonor. If a man therefore purge himself from these, he shall be a vessel unto honor, sanctified, and meet for the master's use, and prepared unto every good work."*

This is an exciting passage. Think of it this way: in a mansion you will find a wide array of various types of dishware. Expensive crystal and china are used for the most special occasions. Then there are nice dishes for everyday use. Next there are some plain, common, plastic dishes for rough usage. Then there are the paper plates, then the dog dish, and finally, the garbage can. The point of II Timothy 2:20–21 is that if we cleanse our lives of what is common and dishonorable, we will be clean, useful, and prepared for the work God has for us. We will be the crystal and china—ready for the Master's special purposes!

How does this relate to marriage? Well, God is continually raising up new generations of men and women who are His servants, through whom He is accomplishing His work in the world. Even though they probably won't make the history books, they will be the truly great people in the world—and they will be in God's history book! They are men and women of faith like the ones mentioned in Hebrews 11. And in every generation, God is raising up a new host of these influential servants.

These "great" men whom the Lord is preparing for His important work need "great" wives—wives who are qualified to be their helpmeets. Likewise, there are also women who have prepared. They are godly, skilled, and zealous. They have strong testimonies. They are excited about the Lord and ready to serve. These women need "great" leaders! Whom do you think God is going to team together? God wants to give *great wives* to *great men*. Therefore, maybe we could summarize it this way: *the way to find a mate is not to look, but to prepare!*

Focus on Ministry

In addition to preparing ourselves, we should also be concentrating on the work God has currently given us to do. We have already discussed this in chapter eight. Matthew 6:33 tells us to seek first God's kingdom and His righteousness. If we focus on these things, He will add to our lives all the other things we need.

COUPLES I'VE OBSERVED

I could tell you dozens of stories of young people I know who did not follow the world's system of dating. As they waited on the Lord, they experienced God's miraculous hand in uniting them with their life partners. For example, a friend of mine, LeAnne, really wanted to get married. She hoped to find someone during her four years at a Christian college, but she graduated without her "Mrs." degree. As much as she wanted to be married, LeAnne desired even more to serve the Lord. She felt called to be a missionary in China. But how will you find a husband in China? She certainly wondered! Nevertheless, she was committed to obeying the Lord and left for the mission field. After a number of years in China, the Lord brought her to Mr. Right—another missionary who was also from the United States. They continue to serve the Lord faithfully. LeAnne put God's work first, and He took care of everything else.

A second friend of mine, Beth, went to a Christian college. Even though Beth majored in elementary education, she said that what she really wanted to do was to get married and raise a family. She had purposed not to date, but to simply wait for the Lord to bring the right man into her life. During her four years at school she received quite a few questions and arguments from other students who tried to convince her of the benefits of dating. Yet, Beth chose to wait.

By the time she graduated, there was still no young man in her life. How would she find a husband now? Shortly after her graduation from college, she was asked to be a bridesmaid in a friend's wedding. At the wedding rehearsal she noticed a godly young man. He also noticed her. In the weeks that followed he talked on the phone with her father (even though her father was not a believer) as well as with another man whom Beth had asked to be a spiritual authority in her life. Everyone agreed he was the right one for her. They became close friends, fell in love, and were married. Anyone who observes their marriage is encouraged to learn that joyous and wonderful marriages do still exist!

I know of other couples who have met at camps, churches, stores, the foreign mission field, or various other places of ministry. But do not think that you must leave home in order to meet someone. I believe that the very best place for a single young lady to be is at home, under her father's authority and direction. The world's system that encourages a time of "independence" for young ladies is a dangerous and unbiblical idea. It makes the transfer from the "freedom" of singleness to the "responsibilities" of marriage strained and difficult. In our modern culture I realize that it is hard to know how to apply this principle. There are obviously many unique situations. Yet, a young lady will receive rich blessings as she commits to staying under her father's protection until the day her father gives her away to her husband. As always, God's design is what works the best!

So in regard to finding a husband, remember that it is no hard thing for the Creator of the universe to bring people together. He is sovereign and there is no limit to His power. *"Behold I am the Lord, the God of all flesh; is there any thing too hard for Me?"* (Jer. 32:27).

When the Strong Winds Blow

Last week I was on the phone with a sixteen-year-old friend of mine. Our conversation started as a casual, friendly chat, but after a few minutes my friend suddenly opened up and said, "I don't know why, Sarah, but I've been feeling sort of rebellious recently."

"Against your parents?"

"Oh, just against everything ... I don't know, it's kind of hard when all my friends are choosing dresses and getting ready for prom ... I mean, I've already decided that I don't want to date and stuff ... and I know I've made the right decision, but I'm just discouraged. And then last week my mom and I were at the store, and I found a great buy on this really fancy dress, but Mom said I couldn't get it because I'd have nowhere to wear it. And it's true, I can't think of any place that I'd wear it ... I know she's right, but, Sarah—it's hard!"

Have you ever felt this way? Confused about what the Lord is doing in your life? Knowing that you want to do the right thing, but struggling in actually doing it? Feeling alone? Discouraged?

"Lord, this is hard," we say.

"I know," He answers.

"But, Lord, I feel alone," we repeat.

And the Lord says, "I know."

"But, it's hard!"

"Yes, I know."

"But won't You take the loneliness away?"

And the Lord says, "Cling to Me. My arms are open. I'm longing to comfort you. My child, come running into My arms."

And we find the Lord more tender and compassionate than we ever imagined. Our loneliness, our hurts, our needs, and our thirst drive us to Him. As we experience His love in a new way, and the joy that comes from a deeper intimacy with Him, we find that the struggle was worth it. He was right after all. It is only because of His care—it is purely out of His love that He allows the pain. And through it all, He is teaching us what it means to trust Him.

One day Jesus and His disciples climbed into a boat. Soon a violent storm arose and the waves swept over the boat. The disciples were terrified, yet Jesus was asleep. In alarm, they rushed to Him, saying,

"Save us. We perish!" Jesus responded, "Why are ye fearful, O ye of little faith?" Then He rebuked the wind and the sea, and it became completely calm (Mt. 8:23–27).

We often look at our circumstances from an earthly perspective and begin to panic. Just as the disciples did, we fear that God has forgotten about us; we think that things are out of control. We figure that just when we need Him most, He has fallen asleep. Do you know why the disciples did not need to fear? Jesus was the One who had led them into the boat! He who had brought them this far would not forget about them now.

When you see your friends dating or getting married, or you feel left out, do not give in to fear as the disciples did. The Lord has not forgotten about you. When you are following Him, you can be sure that He will direct your paths. He who began a good work in you will most assuredly carry it to completion (Phil. 1:6).

A Step at a Time

This afternoon my friend and I met for lunch, ordered our soup and sandwiches, and sat down at a booth. I am often surprised that despite the different family situations, different weaknesses, and different circumstances of the many young ladies I talk with, their struggles are extremely similar! As my friend and I discussed our daily lives and our walk with the Lord, I was reminded of this once again.

The things you struggle with are the same things many other young ladies are also struggling with. Your fears, your hurts, your trials, and your frustrations are the same ones that girls around the world face. Oftentimes we feel alone and think we are the only ones who have ever faced a particular problem, not realizing that countless other girls have the same questions.

Yes, we all have struggles, but the important question is this: how are we responding to the difficulties we are facing in life? It is our response to struggles that will make the difference between being an average young lady or truly being a bright light for Christ. Everyone struggles, but only a few allow their longings, their hurts, and their needs to turn them to God. Only a few take the hard route of humility and honor their parents. Only a few realize the value of each day and use their youth to serve the Lord.

As day by day and minute by minute, we choose to make right decisions and obey the Lord, we are growing, we are becoming more like Jesus, and our faith is being strengthened. We don't just wake up one morning and find that we have become a godly woman or that the Lord has used us to bring forth much fruit. It happens step by step as we obey in each little area.

On the other hand, if day after day we allow compromises, soft decisions, and "little" sins into our lives, we need to stop and recognize what direction we are headed. If we wake up one morning and find that we have fallen into serious sin, we can know that the failure is the result of many small compromises that were happening little by little as we refused to listen to the Lord's promptings and obey His voice.

I am encouraged to hear the many testimonies from young ladies across the country who are making courageous decisions to honor Christ. I know the Lord will bless you richly as you press on to higher ground! Be encouraged. Your work will be rewarded!

Suggested Memory Verse:

"Now unto Him that is able to do exceeding abundantly above all that we ask or think, according to the power that worketh in us, unto Him be glory in the church by Christ Jesus throughout all ages, world without end. Amen." (Ephesians 3:20–21)

Suggested Assignment:

Ask your mother (or another godly lady if necessary) if she would be willing to share some specific advice to help you prepare to be a wife and mother. Here are some questions that would be good to ask her:

1. In what ways do you wish you had been better prepared for marriage and motherhood?
2. What is one specific trait of godliness (patience, joyfulness, kindness, orderliness, etc.) in which you think it would be important for me to improve before I get married?
3. What is one specific household skill that you suggest I learn and develop during this season of my life?

After Years of Imagining

The sun was warm and everything was breezy and peaceful. The princess was as happy as ever. Do you know those days when everything is sunny, both outdoors and in your heart? When the singing of the birds makes your heart do the same? When the beauty of the flowers blooming makes your heart rejoice in what the Master has provided? It was that kind of day for the princess.

She was returning from one of her frequent trips to the various villages where she joyfully and kindly met the needs of many who were fainthearted, poor, injured, and troubled. Today she had paid a special visit to her friend Maiden Flirtelia and given counsel and

encouragement to a girl named Simplicity whom she had met along the way. She also visited a sick mother and played with her children, gave some fabric to a needy family, and delivered a personal letter from her father to a village nobleman. The princess was learning again and again that it is more blessed to give than to receive. The more she delighted in her heavenly Prince, the more she wanted to share with others the fulfillment she had in Him.

As she neared the castle, she saw someone on the road in front of her. It was her father. He seemed to be waiting for her. She quickened Victory's pace a little, wondering if something was wrong. But her father calmly assured her that all was well and asked if he could walk her home. She dismounted, and as they walked with Victory at their side, the princess began to tell him about her day. Her father, however, did not seem to be listening.

The princess looked at him suspiciously and asked, "Father, are you sure that nothing is wrong? ... Father? Why are you smiling like that?"

"My daughter," he said, ignoring her questions, "what shall I say when one of the young men of the kingdom cometh to me to inquire about thy hand? There will be many young men at the summer contest. I would not be surprised to receive such requests."

"Father, it seems that many young men seek only that which will bring pleasure or money. Some be good men, but they have not vision for the greater tasks, neither are they willing to make the sacrifices that such tasks demand. Also, they often be proud and seek their own glory." She thought for a moment and then continued, "It bothers me sometimes when I observe the young men in the kingdom. Do any understand the true battles of our day? Do any fight the good fight? It is this, not noble birth, that is true nobility."

"Father," the princess asked with a small smile, "be there any who have already inquired?"

Attempting to conceal his own enthusiasm, the king proceeded with another question. "My daughter, thou knowest the knight, Sir Valiant?"

The princess felt a shiver surge through her. "Yes, thou knowest I have met him several times."

"What thinkest thou of him?" he asked calmly, rubbing his chin.

"Father, I have tried not to think of him—not because he is undesirable, but maybe because he is too desirable. I do not want to be distracted or consumed with that which is simply a dream."

"But what thinkest thou of him?" the king asked again.

"Of what I know he is true, he is kind-hearted, and ... and he is becoming." The princess tried to read the expression on her father's face, yet continued, "I have been impressed with everything I have seen of him. I have never talked with him at length, Father, but I have wanted to ... How well do you know him?"

"Well, my fair one, your mother and I have been observing him and discussing his character. He indeed has conviction and is steadfast. He knows the battles we face and is a most zealous and faithful subject."

The king paused as if thinking about what to say next. The princess looked up at him intently. Her heart was beating fast, and her mind was racing.

At last the king continued, "Of late, Sir Valiant hath been asking about thee more and more. I do not want to encourage the matter if thou be not truly interested."

Stunned, the princess tried to respond. In reality, she had thought of him countless times since the day they met in the courtyard, and although she had spent such little time with him, she already knew he was the type of man that she dreamed of marrying. Now, with tears in her eyes, she learned that he had noticed her as well.

Sir Valiant had been courageously fighting the king's battles— battles of righteousness and justice. Battles against the false ways that destroy any kingdom that embraces them. In so doing, he had earned himself both respect and honor in the eyes of all—including the king. The Master Matchmaker knew the time had come. Sir Valiant needed a bride who was prepared, zealous, and capable to work hand in hand with him. This bride was already prepared. For in God's perfect way, with love and constant care, through a flawless plan including struggles and lessons, tears and joys, He had prepared for Valiant exactly the right wife. And with the same love and orchestration, the Master Matchmaker had prepared for the princess exactly the right husband. Now at last, at the perfect time, He brought them together.

Epilogue: After Years of Imagining

Her father continued to tell her of his conversation with Sir Valiant. As the princess listened, her eyes began to sparkle and her steps were quick and light with energy. When they arrived at the bridge, the king said he would deliver Victory to the stable hand and then meet her in the garden. He went ahead through the archway, leaving the princess alone to think for a few moments.

She was staring across the fields when she heard the familiar voice below. "I say, Princess, what captures the thoughts of my lovely one this beautiful day?"

"I was thinking of how our Father in heaven perfectly arranges the times and seasons, and provides so wonderfully for those who wait for Him!" she answered.

"Why speak ye such words when He has not yet provided for thee, my single little friend? Art not thou destined to loneliness?"

"Mr. Alligator, is there not only one of thyself also?" countered the princess. "And it be a good thing, I must say!" she added emphatically.

"My, thou art fiery today. But nay, I have a large and renowned family, prominent from ancient times—and influential even today."

"Yea, and I think I know of some of them. I believe you had a cousin who lived in a garden and another who has even of recent times been visiting villages not far away. I must go. I have much to do and I need not thy advice."

"I wonder what she meant about my cousin?" the alligator muttered to himself as he watched her run through the archway into the court garden.

The princess caught up with her father and together they walked straight through the garden and the main hall to the front brick porch, talking about Sir Valiant as they went. Truthfully, they had talked about him before on numerous occasions, but not with knowledge of his interest. Now everything was changed and floods of new thoughts streamed into the princess's mind. Then, as they entered the outer court, the princess stopped in her tracks and stood speechless in the middle of a sentence. She found herself face to face with the one who had just been absorbing all her thoughts.

Sir Valiant, himself seemingly taken by surprise, expecting only her father to return, was also unable to speak. The princess, beaming with excitement, was more beautiful than he had remembered. With all his rehearsed words fleeing from him, he stood in fear and was hardly able to do anything but smile.

* * *

The day of the summer contest arrived, and it proved to be a most successful event! The whole affair was festive and entertaining, with impressive talent displayed by many a knight.

Even though the event was not for the hand of the princess, nevertheless much attention was given her and, among the young men, talk of her was not a little. It was, therefore, an immense surprise when it was revealed that the king would announce the courtship of his daughter on the morrow at the concluding feast on the castle lawn. The festivities and joyful spirit rose in a crescendo as the time drew near. With much pomp and drama, the king finally addressed the throng. In kind and humble words he commended the people, especially the young men who had competed. The king gave unexpected prizes to many, recognizing not just courage and skill, but also character and service. The royal silver sword was given to Sir Honor, a knight whom everyone agreed had outshined the others. Then the king spoke of his role as a father, as well as the wonder of the heavenly Father who always arranges matters according to His miraculous design.

Finally, he announced the news everyone was waiting to hear. Sir Valiant had won the heart of the princess! Not with talent or skill, not with words or money, not with bravery or nobility, but with a heart that was pure and a life that was true. The king was careful not to offend the other knights as he applauded the character and strength of Sir Valiant. Rather, he challenged and encouraged everyone to follow the way of truth, reminding them that God is always faithful to reward the righteous.

* * *

The moon was bright and a cool breeze kissed the cheeks of the princess and Sir Valiant as they sat talking in the royal garden. They had just arrived home from their honeymoon, and although they were a little worn out from the trip, they were as excited as ever. It was a peaceful evening, with no noise but the crickets chirping and the leaves rustling in the wind.

"Why did you not seek a wife sooner than you did?" the princess asked, breaking the silence.

"I felt it was my duty to finish some assignments that required danger, much mobility, and considerable time. Also, I never met one who was committed to the same tasks as myself—until I met you."

"Yes, God's timing was right," the princess acknowledged, "but it was hard to wait. I used to have long talks with my father."

"And so did I," replied Sir Valiant. "I feared each time I came to the castle that there would be news of thy courtship or marriage. Yet I, too, felt I could do nothing until I finished my mission—and until I knew more of you. Also, I was afraid. I had seen battle, I had endured pain, I had been near the claws of death without fear. But approaching thy father for thy hand? Nay, this struck fear in my heart. There was much to lose if he said no. It took much time—many seasons for the Lord to prepare me. But such was good. It was needful."

"I remember the first time I saw you making a proclamation with a company of knights in the village," the princess said sweetly. "You were different from the other knights. Youthful—and yet you had a confidence and maturity because you were concerned with higher matters than they. You seemed to have a mission unlike the other knights. Do you remember your thoughts the first time we met?"

Sir Valiant gazed at the bright moon and recalled, "I was interested in you the first time I saw you. And I knew by the sparkle and brightness in thine eyes that thou wast a servant of the King of Kings. I began to converse with thy father, but mostly about business and only a little about his daughter—and then only simple questions that anyone would ask. I was afraid to show direct interest. After all, who was I but a mere knight? Not a noble or lord. I talked more to our heavenly Father than to your father. And of course, I discussed the matter often with my parents as well. Due to the assignments that the king gave me, I had more and more occasion to communicate with him and each time to learn a little more of thee."

"What is something thou heardest of me in those days?" inquired the princess.

Sir Valiant thought briefly and laughed. "I encountered a certain one who told me thou wast foolish and naïve."

"Foolish and naïve!? Someone said that? Did you believe this one?"

"Yea, I did, because that same one told me that you had turned down a certain Sir Eloquence because he was not of true character. Then I knew that thou wast foolish and naïve indeed, but that thy foolishness was wisdom and that thou wast naïve only to the world's error. I had respect for thee, for few maidens would have chosen such."

"And who was it who gave of me this report?" she asked.

"Know ye not? Thou spakest with him often. He claimed to be thy wise counselor."

The princess laughed. "I remember those talks well. The alligator seemed to always be attacking with doubts and fears. It was a difficult time for me, as I often felt lonely and was forced to walk by faith, facing an unknown future. But it was during that period that I truly fell in love with our heavenly Father. I would not trade that for anything."

"Nor would I want you to be any other way."

The princess snuggled close as Valiant continued, "Do you remember our first few months getting to know each other? Everything was so new."

"How could I ever forget?" she spoke softly. "Everything was a first. I think that is what made it so special. I had never been in love before. It was so new and pure. It was like being on a treasure hunt with unending treasure or being in a new land with all kinds of wonderful places to explore."

"I remember our very first candlelight dinner. I could hardly believe it was actually happening," Sir Valiant said. "But do you know what my favorite part of our courtship was? It was our long talks as we sat here in the garden and walked on the forest trails. The time would pass so quickly. And the hours we spent praying and serving the Lord together drew our hearts closer and closer."

"Yes, like the day we went to the village together for the first time," the princess mentioned. "I respected the way you worked with

the people. I was challenged to see your dedication to our heavenly Father's business, and I wanted to be your helper."

The princess noticed how many stars had appeared and how very quiet it was. The chirping of the crickets had ceased. After several moments of silence the princess said, "I often think of the first letter you sent me. I was overjoyed. I read and re-read it until it was memorized. I had never received a love letter before."

"Yes, you had," Valiant reminded her with a grin.

The princess smiled. "That is true... I have a long letter from my heavenly Prince. I'm still studying that one. Indeed, do you not think that all of our experiences were sweeter because we had learned first of all to fall in love with our heavenly Father?"

The princess did not give him time to respond but continued her contemplation. "When I woke up on the day of our wedding, I almost thought I was in a beautiful dream that could not possibly be true. The day seemed perfect in every way. After years of imagining what it would be like and wondering if it would ever happen, here I was gazing into the eyes of the one God had provided. You gave me the most precious gifts—thy heart, thy purity, and thy first kiss. And by God's grace, I was able to give thee the same. Truly, these were the best gifts either of us could have asked for." She spoke almost in a whisper as she leaned back into the arms of Sir Valiant and slipped her hand in his. A tear of joy fell softly upon her cheek as she pondered the goodness of her heavenly Prince.

In reality, it would not be honest for me to say that the dreams of the princess had come true. It was not her dream, but God's perfect plan—which far surpassed her own dreams—that had come to pass in God's time and in God's way. The journey may have been narrow and difficult, but the wedding day was a testimony to the entire kingdom. The king and queen gave their full blessing on the marriage, and the whole kingdom celebrated. The princess had saved herself fully for one man, and with unspeakable joy she declared that it was worth the wait. She understood that new challenges lay ahead, but she also knew that He who had been faithful through every past struggle would continue to be faithful through the next.

Not only had the couple gained the conditions for the very best and happiest marriage, they had also gained a good testimony—one that was observed and proclaimed throughout the kingdom far and wide. Because of their sacrifices, many other young maidens and squires chose to follow the example of Sir Valiant and his bride.

And the alligator? Well, he was not invited to the wedding.

Before You Meet Prince Charming

How to Become a Princess

A true princess is a daughter of a true king. A princess doesn't have to do anything at all to become a princess—just be born. It may take her many years before she learns to act like a princess, but she is already the daughter of the king.

God is the King of Kings. Therefore, every one of His daughters is a true princess. Are you one of His children? Have you been born into His family? If so, then you are a true princess. And the Almighty King is your Father.

Isn't Every Girl on Earth a Princess?

After all, God created all of us, right? Yes, He did. But we have sinned and turned away from Him. Every one of us has broken His righteous laws. None of us deserve to be in His family. We are all disqualified.

God loves us and wants us to be with Him forever. And yet, though He desires to forgive us, He is just. He must punish sin. That's why Jesus came. He—being God—became man, lived a sinless life, and died a horrible death, taking the punishment for our sin. God carried out justice by punishing Jesus instead of us. Then Christ rose again, conquering death—and is now in heaven preparing a place for us.

Jesus Christ now offers forgiveness and eternal life to any who will come to Him. Even though He desires that every girl on earth be in His family, He doesn't force anyone. Rather, He gives each person a choice. Very sadly, many choose to reject the free gift of eternal life which He offers. Therefore, no, every girl is not a true princess. Only those who turn to Christ—this is the point of spiritual birth.

Satan's Deadly Lie

This leads to another important concept. A princess is not a princess because of how she acts but because she was born to the king. In the same way, we are not children of God because of our own good works, but only because God in His mercy has invited us to be born into His family. As the alligator spoke lies to the princess, so there is an enemy speaking lies to the world. One of his biggest, most attractive, and most convincing lies is that *good people go to heaven*. This is false. Only two kinds of people go to heaven: 1) perfect people (of which there are none, but Christ). And 2) sinners who have been forgiven. No one can possibly meet God's righteous standards on his own. No one can ever be good enough. It is not by going to church, doing good works, being baptized, or becoming religious that any of us may enter heaven. Eternal life is a gift. It is not something that we earn. Acting like a princess could never be enough. We have to be born into God's family.

How Does One Enter God's Family?

It's very simple. John 1:11-12 says, *"He came to His own, and those who were His own did not receive Him. But as many as received Him, to them He gave the right to become children of God, even to those who believe in His name"* (NASB). Jesus already did the work. He paid the ultimate price. He asks us simply to receive Him, to believe in Him as Lord, to accept Him as our Savior.

Let's look at it this way: when we were born physically, we entered into our earthly family. In the same way, we must be born spiritually in order to enter God's family. Jesus said to Nicodemus in John 3, *"Verily, verily, I say unto thee, Except a man be born again, he cannot see the kingdom of God."* Jesus goes on to explain how this happens: *"For God so loved the world, that He gave His only begotten Son, that whosoever believeth in Him should not perish, but have everlasting life."*

It is important to understand that there are two kinds of people in the world—those who are part of God's family and those who are not. In which category are you? Can you point to a time in your life when you accepted Christ as your Savior and entered into God's family?

If not, or if you are unsure, now is the time to become sure. Acknowledge your sin. Acknowledge that you deserve hell. Receive Christ into your life. Ask Him to save you. Request the free gift of eternal life that He wants to give you.

He promises to save all who call upon His name (Rom. 10:9-13). By putting your faith in God's promises, you can know that you are His daughter—a true princess indeed!

The Story of Bright Lights

TRAINING YOUNG LADIES TO BE RADIANT IN GODLINESS, HOLINESS, AND TESTIMONY

Bright Lights began in May of 1996. I was seventeen at the time and concerned about the lives of many young ladies I knew. The Lord had given me a desire to begin a discipleship ministry with younger girls and to share with them some of the things that He had done in my life. I decided to call the group Bright Lights. Bright stands for Being Radiant In Godliness, Holiness, and Testimony.

We started meeting regularly for times of practical teaching, testimonies, accountability, reading biographies, activities, singing, tea, dessert, and fellowship. The Lord continued to bring more and more girls to our Bright Lights group, and we were thrilled to see Him working in our lives.

Bright Lights began for girls ages ten to thirteen. These important years are just before the fork in the road when young people make choices about which direction they will go. The goal of Bright Lights is to give young ladies the training and preparation they need so that they can make it through their teenage years strong for the Lord without rebellion or failure. Our desire and prayer is that Bright Lights would be a group with *positive* peer pressure—where girls would be lifted up by godly fellowship rather than pulled down by negative influences.

I soon found out that many parents were worried about their daughters and looking for good fellowship for them. One mother told me, "Bright Lights was just what our daughter needed at that time in her life." Another explained that she appreciated Bright Lights because it reinforced the same things she was trying to teach at home. "My daughter responds especially well when another older girl is teaching it," I was told. A father said, "When our daughter gets home from Bright Lights, she calls the whole family together and teaches all of us the things she learned." I was excited when I saw girls begin to make commitments to stay under their parents' authority, to clear their conscience, to spend time in God's Word everyday, to minister to their siblings, and to use their teenage years for the Lord.

MORE GROUPS STARTING

As my Bright Lights group continued to grow, I began getting questions from other older girls and mothers who wanted to lead groups for young ladies. They asked if I would share with them what I had done in Bright Lights. I found that many had the same vision for working with young ladies and were looking for ideas and resources. At the same time, I was receiving comments from mothers who would say, "Oh, if only we had something like this in our area. This is just what our daughter needs."

I began to pray that the Lord would raise up other young ladies to lead groups. Then I started thinking about how I could help others and pass on to them the things I had learned from leading Bright Lights. My dad encouraged me to hold a Leaders Training Conference. The first one was in May of 1999, and we have continued to hold Leaders Training Conferences about once a year.

These four-day conferences have been very encouraging for me as I see the quality and enthusiasm of the girls who come, their heart for ministry, and their ideas. The conference includes sessions on *How to Start a Bright Lights group, Principles of Ministry, Practical Ways to Reach the Hearts of Young Ladies, Being a Bright Light, How to Lead an Effective Bright Lights Meeting, Rewards and Demands of the Ministry,* other various sessions, and "hands-on" experience leading an actual Bright Lights meeting. A Leaders Training kit is available for young ladies who would like to start a Bright Lights group but are not able to come to a conference. Also, notebooks, lessons, and other resources are available for the girls who would be in those groups. As of fall 2007, there are over 200 Bright Lights groups that have started in thirty-five different states.

I believe that we as young ladies often underestimate the impact that we have on girls who look up to us. We have a tremendous opportunity and responsibility to set a godly example and to invest in their lives. Leading a Bright Lights group is a way to pass on to younger girls the things that God has been teaching you. Though there are many important avenues of ministry, Bright Lights will give experience in the most fundamental element of ministry—how to "disciple." Also, by teaching these foundations of spiritual strength you yourself will be strengthened. Teaching something always causes the teacher to learn more than the students.

MOTHER/DAUGHTER CONFERENCES

As the girls in my Bright Lights group grew older, we began to pray that the Lord would give us, as a group, opportunities to reach more young ladies. In the spring of 2001, about fifteen of the older girls and I decided to host a Strong in the Lord Conference in order to challenge and encourage young ladies to live for the Lord. Through skits, testimonies, stories, and small group teaching, we covered topics such as *Being Strong for the Lord in Your Youth*, *Keeping a Clear Conscience*, *Giving Your Heart to Your Parents*, and *Making Brothers and Sisters Best Friends*.

We never would have expected that the Lord was beginning a whole new aspect of the Bright Lights ministry! But over the years, He has been opening doors for us to continue to host Strong in the Lord Conferences for thousands of mothers and daughters across the nation and in other countries. We now also teach Radiant Purity Conferences for girls ages 12 and up and their parents, covering many of the topics which are taught in this book. See p. 257-258 for more information.

More conferences are being planned, more groups are starting, more material is being developed, and we are looking forward to seeing what the Lord has in store for us. I am very thankful for all I have learned from leading Bright Lights—I'm sure I have learned the most! And I praise the Lord for all the young ladies He is raising up who are bright lights for Him. There is a great need for more of them in this generation of darkness.

FOR MORE INFORMATION

For information about groups or conferences in your area, or to order the Bright Lights material, see *www.brightlights.info*.

If you or your mother would like more information about how to begin a Bright Lights group in your area, we would be happy to send you a complimentary ten-minute DVD. Simply send $2.50 for shipping and handling and a request for the Bright Lights informational packet to:

Bright Lights
PO Box 11451
Cedar Rapids, IA
52410-1451

Strong in the Lord Conference

For mothers and daughters, ages 8-14.
*These weekend conferences are taught by Sarah Mally
and the Bright Lights Staff*

PURPOSE OF CONFERENCE:

To encourage young ladies to seek the Lord with all their heart; to prepare young ladies to be strong for the Lord all the way through their teen years and avoid the traps that many teens fall into; and to provide these girls with the friendship, fellowship, and godly influence of young ladies who are bright lights for the Lord

TOPICS INCLUDED:

Preparing to Stay Strong for the Lord through Your Youth
Making Brothers and Sisters Best Friends
How to Turn Your Heart to Your Parents
Contentment and Trusting God
How to Keep Your Heart Pure From Polluting Influences
Developing a Disciplined Walk With God
Being a Bright Light to Those Around You

ALSO INCLUDED:

Humorous and insightful skits, personal testimonies, a chalk talk, small group discussions and activities, singing, and harp music

MORE INFORMATION:

If you would like to attend a Strong in the Lord conference or if you would like to host one in your area, please see *www.brightlights.info* or e-mail *conference@brightlights.info*.

Radiant Purity Conference

For mothers and daughters, ages 12-24.
These weekend conferences are taught by Sarah Mally and the
Bright Lights Staff

ABOUT THE CONFERENCE:

A young lady who is pure shines with a radiant brightness in this world of darkness. How can a girl stay physically and emotionally pure as she waits for God's best in marriage?

This conference will encourage young ladies to guard their hearts and minds, to desire the very best marriage, to give their hearts to their father, to avoid the dangers of the world's thinking, to delight in Jesus, and to use their years of singleness for the Lord.

Creatively presented through stories and testimonies, practical instruction, skits, and real-life examples, this conference gives Biblical answers to everyday questions and deep life struggles. It also deals with many practical topics such as modesty and how to guard your heart when you have a crush. The material is discreet and appropriate for 12 year olds and yet relevant to all ages. Also includes testimonies from young ladies who serve as Bright Lights staff, chalk drawings, and harp music.

MORE INFORMATION:

If you would like to attend a Radiant Purity conference or if you would like to host one in your area, please see *www.brightlights.info* or e-mail us at *conference@radiantpurity.com*

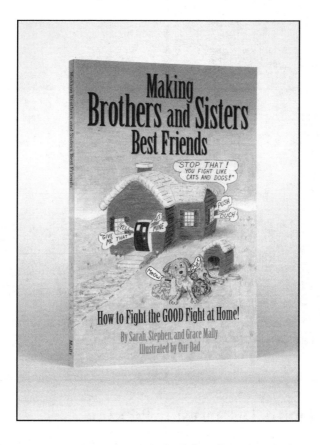

MAKING BROTHERS AND SISTERS BEST FRIENDS

The emphasis of this book is not merely "getting along" with brothers and sisters, but making them best friends. Every chapter contains a section by Sarah, Stephen, and Grace—giving the book three perspectives and three personalities. Including humor, personal stories, cartoons, and practical ideas, this book challenges families to work through pride, offenses, and irritations in their relationships and learn to become best friends. Available in English and Spanish.

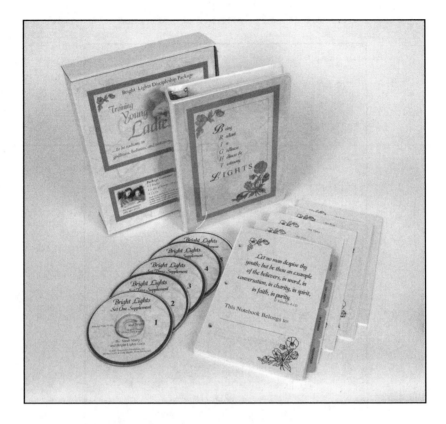

BRIGHT LIGHTS DISCIPLESHIP PACKAGE

This discipleship course is recommended for use in a Bright Lights group, a small group setting, or for young ladies and mothers to read and discuss together. Covering fundamental areas such as developing a close relationship with your parents, contentment, discernment, accepting the way God designed you, how to develop a ministry, controlling your words, choosing wise friends, and many other practical topics, this course is designed to encourage young ladies to use their teen years for the Lord. Each illustrated lesson contains rich biblical insights, practical applications, and testimonies from girls who share how the Lord has been working in their lives. Package includes one Bright Lights binder, Sets 1-5 (29 eight-page booklets), and 5 CDs which contain stories and testimonies.

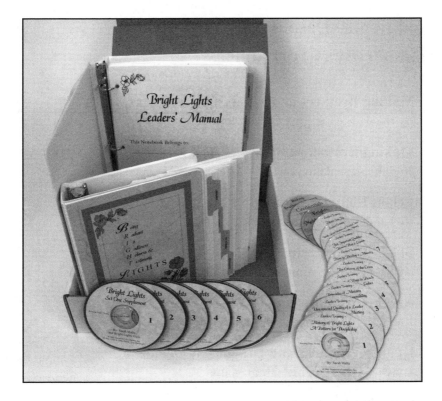

BRIGHT LIGHTS LEADERS TRAINING KIT

This kit was developed to provide encouragement, training, ideas, and resources for young ladies or mothers who would like to begin a discipleship group for girls in their area. It includes the full Bright Lights curriculum (see previous page) and a Leaders Manual with ideas and supplements for the teacher. The kit also includes twelve CDs of the sessions from the Leaders Training conference, covering topics such as principles of ministry, how to lead an effective Bright Lights meeting, insights on discipleship, and practical ways to reach the hearts of young ladies.

Additional Resources from Tomorrow's Forefathers

Making Brothers and Sisters Best Friends (book)
By Sarah, Stephen and Grace Mally (272 pages)

Making Brothers and Sisters Best Friends CD or DVD
50 min. presentation by Sarah, Stephen, and Grace Mally

Bright Lights Discipleship Package
By Sarah Mally (Binder, 5 sets, 5 CDs)

Bright Lights Leaders Training Kit
By Sarah Mally (complete curriculum, and leadership material)

Knights, Maidens and Dragons CD or DVD
1 hr. presentation by Harold and Sarah Mally

Knights, Maidens and Dragons Supplement
Sixty page booklet by Harold Mally

Learning From Dad
Father-led series to train the family in godliness by Harold Mally

Preparing Young Ladies for Their Teen Years CD
1 hr. presentation by Sarah Mally

Raising Pure Daughters in a Generation of Darkness
50 min. presentation by Sarah Mally

Credentials Without College CD
1 hr. presentation by Sarah and Stephen Mally

Tomorrow's Forefathers, Inc.
PO Box 11451
Cedar Rapids, Iowa 52410-1451
www.tomorrowsforefathers.com
info@tomorrowsforefathers.com

About the Author

Sarah Mally is a single young woman with a heart for young ladies. She is the founder of Bright Lights, a discipleship ministry designed to equip young ladies to use the years of their youth fully for Christ. This ministry which began in her living room has now expanded across the nation and in several other countries. As of fall 2007, over 200 groups have started in thirty-five different states and 5 countries. Bright Lights hosts Strong in the Lord conferences for mothers and daughters, trains and equips leaders of Bright Lights groups, and provides discipleship material for young ladies. Sarah and her family speak often at churches and homeschool conferences. In 2002, Sarah and her younger brother and sister published the book, *Making Brothers and Sisters Best Friends,* which has sold over 40,000 copies.

To Contact the Author:

Sarah Mally
PO Box 11451
Cedar Rapids, IA 52410-1451
info@radiantpurity.com
www.radiantpurity.com